NOT-FOR-PROFIT ACCOUNTING MADE EASY

Warren Ruppel, CPA

John Wiley & Sons, Inc.

Library of Congress Cataloging-in-Publication Data:

Ruppel, Warren.
    Not-for-profit accounting made easy / Warren Ruppel.
        p.   cm.
    ISBN 0-471-20679-2
    1. Nonprofit organizations—United States—Accounting.   2. Financial statements—United States.   I. Title.
    HF5686.N56 R86 2002
    657'.98—dc21

                                                                2001008391

Contents

About the Author

Warren Ruppel, CPA, has over 20 years of expertise in not-for-profit and governmental accounting. He currently is the Assistant Comptroller for Accounting of the City of New York, where he is responsible for all aspects of the city's accounting and financial reporting. He began his career at KPMG Peat Marwick after graduating from St. John's University, New York. He later jointed Deloitte & Touche to specialize in audits of not-for-profit organizations and governments. Mr. Ruppel has also served as the chief financial officer of an international not-for-profit organization and as a partner in a small CPA practice.

Mr. Ruppel has served as instructor for many training courses, including specialized governmental and not-for-profit programs and seminars. He has also been an adjunct lecturer of accounting at the Bernard M. Baruch College of the City University of New York. He is the author of three other books, *OMB Circular A-133 Audits, Not-for-Profit Organization Audits,* and Wiley's *GAAP for Governments.*

Mr. Ruppel is a member of the American Institute of Certified Public Accountants as well as the New York State Society of Certified Public Accountants, where he serves on the Governmental Accounting and Auditing and Not-for-Profit Organizations Committees. He is also a member of the Institute of Management Accountants and is a past president of the New York Chapter. Mr. Ruppel is a member of the Government Finance Officers Association and serves on its Special Review Committee.

Preface

Not-for-Profit Accounting Made Easy is a plain-language, easy to understand explanation of the various accounting and financial reporting practices of not-for-profit organizations. It is designed for all those individuals who have contact with these organizations—management and staff, board members, consultants, donors, creditors—who should understand not-for-profit accounting but often do not. It is written for the non-accountant, but those accountants who are unfamiliar with the nuances of not-for-profit accounting (or those who have grown a little rusty in the latest accounting pronouncements) and do not need an in-depth technical volume will also find it useful.

There are over one million not-for-profit organizations in the United States. They exist in all sizes and for many purposes. They range from homeless shelters to country clubs, from child daycare centers to colleges and universities, from local to international. One thing these organizations all have in common is that their finances are subject to a great deal of scrutiny. Effective accounting and financial reporting is a key ingredient in withstanding this scrutiny and ensuring accountability. Having a basic understanding of not-for-profit accounting and financial reporting can be a real asset for the many people who have contact with not-for-profit organizations in many different ways. This book may not make you love not-for-profit accounting, but it will teach you the basics and help you read and understand a set of not-for-profit financial statements.

My thanks to all those at John Wiley & Sons, Inc., who helped make this book a reality, particularly John DeRemigis who supported and nurtured the concept and Louise Jacob for making sure that the book is a quality product. Thanks also to my family, my wife Marie and sons Christopher and Gregory, for their love and support throughout the project.

Warren Ruppel, CPA

New York, New York
January, 2002

CHAPTER 1

Understanding the Basics of Not-for-Profit Accounting

This chapter provides some very basic information about not-for-profit accounting to provide a basis for understanding the principles and standards that are discussed in greater detail throughout the remainder of this book. A lack of understanding or misunderstanding of these fundamentals will cause the reader to be lost when trying to understand more complex principles. Specifically, this chapter will:

- Identify generally accepted accounting principles.
- Define and give examples of assets, liabilities, net assets, revenues, and expenses usually found in not-for-profit organizations' financial statements.
- Explain what is meant by the accrual basis of accounting. How does this differ from the cash basis of accounting, and which is better?
- Describe what happened to fund accounting.

WHAT ARE GENERALLY ACCEPTED ACCOUNTING PRINCIPLES?

Non-accountants sometimes ask the question, "Well, if these accounting principles are only generally accepted, that must mean that there are other perfectly good accounting principles that have less than general acceptance that are fine to use." Unfortunately for those desiring creativity and uniqueness in their accounting principles, this is not the case. Generally accepted accounting principles (GAAP) are the rules of road that need to be followed by not-for-profit organizations if they want to proclaim that their financial statements are prepared in accordance with GAAP.

WHY IS PREPARING GAAP FINANCIAL STATEMENTS IMPORTANT?

Sometimes not-for-profit organizations are required by law or regulation to prepare financial statements in accordance with GAAP. Most states require that not-for-profit organizations that are organized within a state (or raise funds within that state) file an annual report with the state charities bureau (or its equivalent) and, for all but the smallest not-for-profit organizations, the annual reports usually require that financial statements prepared in accordance with GAAP be included with the annual report.

Several other groups are also fond of financial statements prepared in accordance with GAAP. Large, sophisticated donors often request copies of an organization's financial statements, and having these financial statements prepared in accordance with GAAP lends a high degree of credibility to the financial statements. Creditors that loan money or provide credit lines to not-for-profit organizations also like to see GAAP financial statements. Sometimes a significant vendor or contractor will also request financial statements of the organization, particularly when a long-term lease or equipment-financing contract is being executed. Having financial statements prepared in accordance with GAAP makes them more understandable, comparable with other not-for-profit organizations, and provides a better representation of the financial affairs of the not-for-profit organization. Additionally, if the not-for-profit organization provides services to a governmental organization (federal, state, city, school district, county, etc.), the contract with the governmental entity often requires that financial statements prepared in accordance with GAAP be submitted to the government every year.

Who Sets the Laws of GAAP?

Generally accepted accounting principles for not-for-profit organizations are basically set by the Financial Accounting Standards Board (FASB). The FASB is a private organization that is financially controlled and supported by the Financial Accounting Foundation (FAF), itself a not-for-profit organization. The FAF also oversees the Governmental Accounting Standards Board (GASB), which sets GAAP for governmental entities.

The first level in the GAAP hierarchy, category A, consists of Financial Accounting Standards Board (FASB) Statements of Financial Accounting Standards and Interpretations (as an example, the reader may be familiar with FASB Statement No. 117, which has had a significant impact on financial reporting for not-for-profit organizations and will be discussed throughout this book). Also at the highest level of authority are statements issued by the FASB's predecessor standards-setting organizations, opinions issued by the now-defunct Accounting Principles Board (APB), and Accounting Research Bulletins, which were formerly issued by the American Institute of Certified Public Accountants (AICPA).

The next level in the GAAP hierarchy, category B, consists of FASB Technical Bulletins and, if cleared by the FASB, Industry Audit and Accounting Guides issued by the AICPA and Statements of Position issued by the AICPA.

The third category, category C, consists of AICPA Accounting Standards Executive Committee Practice Bulletins that have been cleared by the FASB and issues resolved by the FASB's Emerging Issues Task Force.

The lowest level in the GAAP hierarchy, category D, consists of AICPA Accounting Interpretations and Implementation Guides published by the FASB staff. Also included in this category are other practices that are widely recognized as prevalent, either generally or as pertain to a specific industry.

While these terms may not mean much to the non-accountant, it is important for the reader to at least be a little familiar with them in order to have an idea of their relative importance, which can come in handy in conversations with a not-for-profit organization's accountants or independent auditors.

Who Makes Sure the Not-for-Profit Organization's Financial Statements Conform with GAAP?

The answer may surprise the non-accountant, but the fair presentation of a not-for-profit organization's financial condition and results of operations in its financial statements prepared in accordance with GAAP is the responsibility of the not-for-profit organization's management. For those who would have guessed this responsibility was that of the not-for-profit organization's independent auditor, a serious change in paradigm needs to be made. Independent auditors are hired to perform an audit and issue an opinion as to whether the financial statements *prepared by management* are presented in accordance with GAAP. Not-for-profit organizations are notorious for passing the responsibility for preparing financial statements off to the independent auditor. The common reason for doing this, particularly in smaller organizations, is that the not-for-profit organization may not have individuals with the technical expertise on staff to take full responsibility for preparing the financial statements. While it is understandable how this happens, the management of the organization is, in fact, responsible for the financial statements. If assistance is needed of the independent auditor, management should at least understand how the financial statements are ultimately prepared and what types of adjustments to the organization's books and records are being made by the independent auditor to result in GAAP financial statements.

It is worth noting, however, that independent auditors take the fact that the financial statements are management's responsibility very seriously. The second sentence of a standard auditor's opinion letter states: "These financial statements are the responsibility of XYZ's management." While this is most assuredly an attempt by independent auditors to limit their legal exposure in case the financial statements actually are not prepared in accordance with GAAP, it does highlight the fact that, the way the system works, the financial statements are management's responsibility.

What Happens If the Financial Statements Are Not in Accordance with GAAP?

It depends. If a not-for-profit organization prepares financial statements that its management believes are in accordance with GAAP while its independent auditor does not believe they are in accordance with GAAP, one of two things can happen:

- *The not-for-profit organization accepts changes to the statements prepared by the auditor and corrects the financial statements.* In this case, both management and the independent auditor now believe the financial statements are prepared in accordance with GAAP. The problem is resolved and the independent auditor issues an unqualified opinion on the financial statements.
- *The not-for-profit organization may disagree with the changes proposed by the auditor.* On the other hand, the independent auditor may propose that an adjustment be made to the financial statements or that additional disclosures be included, but the management of the not-for-profit organization is unable to obtain the necessary information with which to adjust the financial statements. In this case, the auditor will issue a qualified opinion on the financial statements because of the departure from GAAP. This means that the financial statements are prepared in accordance with GAAP, with the exception of the problem item. In some rare cases, if the problem is so serious that it is pervasive and affects the financial statements as a whole, the auditor may issue an adverse opinion on the financial statements.

This means that the financial statements in their entirety are not prepared in accordance with GAAP.

The acceptance of financial statements that are not in accordance with GAAP will vary among the different users of those financial statements. A state charities office may accept financial statements that are qualified for a GAAP exception, but may not accept statements with an adverse opinion. A bank or other creditor may find that any departure from GAAP in a not-for-profit organization's financial statements would be a negative factor in determining whether credit should be granted to the not-for-profit organization.

Tip   A not-for-profit organization may deliberately choose not to use GAAP for its financial statements, but rather an "other comprehensive basis of accounting" (OCBA), such as the cash basis, for the statements. More on this topic will be provided later in this chapter.

The bottom line of this discussion is that GAAP is widely recognized as providing the best information about a not-for-profit organization's financial position and activities. For all but the smallest not-for-profit organizations (which may not even issue financial statements), it is likely that the benefits of having financial statements prepared in accordance with GAAP will outweigh the costs.

Red Flag   Not-for-profit organizations often prepare annual financial statements on a GAAP basis, while providing their board of directors or executive management with financial information on a quarterly basis. The total of all four quarters of these quarterly financial information reports often does not equal amounts reported in financial statements prepared in accordance with GAAP, because there are frequently adjustments made to conform to

GAAP that are only made when the annual financial statements are prepared. Common examples include depreciation expense, bad debt expense, and inventories (each of which will be discussed later in greater detail), which are only recorded annually and not reflected in quarterly financial information.

DEFINITIONS AND EXAMPLES OF ASSETS, LIABILITIES, REVENUES, AND EXPENSES USUALLY FOUND IN NOT-FOR-PROFIT ORGANIZATIONS' FINANCIAL STATEMENTS

In order to understand the basic financial statements of a not-for-profit organization and how various transactions are accounted for under GAAP, the reader needs to understand the various asset, liability, revenue, and expense accounts typically found in the financial statements of not-for-profit organizations. Some accounts are easier to describe (for example, cash) than others (for example, deferred charges). Even with the easier accounts, there are often underlying rules that need to be understood to really comprehend the financial statement item being reported. Using the example of cash, the financial statement reader might be interested in knowing the distinctions between unrestricted cash and restricted cash and how each is reported. The financial statement reader might also be interested in knowing what cash equivalents are, which are sometimes included in the financial statement line item Cash and cash equivalents. The point is that there are any number of nuances and requirements that have developed that determine how items are reported. The following pages describe some of the more common items encountered in not-for-profit financial accounting. (Again, note that this discussion provides only basic rules. Financial statement preparers need to refer to the comprehensive rules found in other sources, such as Wiley's *Not-for-Profit GAAP*, which is written for those requiring a more in-depth understanding of the GAAP requirements.)

Assets

Let us start by looking at the GAAP definition of an asset. FASB Concepts Statement No. 6, "Elements of Financial Statements" (FASBCS 6), defines assets in the following way: "Assets are probable future economic benefits obtained or controlled by a particular entity as a result of past transactions or events." And all this time you thought that assets were stuff that you owned! The fact is, the FASB definition is meant to provide a broader context to assets, rather than a narrower definition that only implies ownership. For example, if a not-for-profit organization prepays its liability insurance premium for the following year, it really does not "own" anything as a result of that prepayment. However, the prepayment will provide a future economic benefit to the not-for-profit organization, which will be insured during the following year without having to pay an insurance premium in that year. Thinking of assets as including things that the organization owns as well as future economic benefits that it is entitled to will help the reader understand what types of items are considered assets.

Note also that assets are measured in financial statements as of a point in time, that is, as of the date of the statement of financial position, which is sometimes referred to as the balance sheet. For example, if the not-for-profit organization's fiscal year-end is June 30, its statement of financial position will report its assets as of that date. Assets are also presented in the statement of financial position in their order of liquidity, which means the assets that can be converted the most readily into cash are reported first. More information on this concept will be presented in Chapter 2.

Some of the types of assets often found on a not-for-profit organization's statement of financial position are:

- Cash
- Cash equivalents
- Investments
- Contributions receivable
- Accounts receivable
- Other receivables

- Inventories
- Property, plant, and equipment
- Prepaid expenses

Cash

Cash is a fairly obvious asset. It represents the balances in the not-for-profit organization's bank accounts. The presentation of cash represents the book balances of the bank accounts, not the amounts reported on the bank statements. The book balances are similar to what individuals keep as balances in their own checkbooks, that is, checks that have been written and deducted from the balance but that have not yet cleared the bank. Similarly, deposits that have been received but have not yet cleared the bank are also included in the balance.

The cash amount reported on the statement of financial position should include:

- *All demand bank accounts that the not-for-profit organization has, including those for general disbursements, payroll imprest accounts, separate accounts for wire transfers, and so forth.* (One cash balance is reported on the financial statements representing the aggregation of all of these accounts.)
- *All petty cash accounts that are maintained by the not-for-profit organization.*

Cash on the statement of financial position should *not* include:

- *Cash that is restricted by some legally enforceable instrument.* Generally, this would include cash maintained in debt service reserve accounts required to be maintained by the related debt instruments. Restricted cash is usually shown as a separate line item in the statement of financial position to make it clear to the reader that it is not available to pay the not-for-profit organization's current bills.
- *Cash that is received and held as a security deposit that will be returned to the provider at the end of some agreement.* For ex-

ample, if a not-for-profit organization rents a part of its office space to another organization and holds a $1,000 security deposit that it collects from the renter, that security deposit cash should not be included in the cash balance of the not-for-profit organization on the statement of financial position.

Cash Equivalents

The term cash equivalents refers to investments that are so close to being realized as cash that they are viewed essentially as the equivalent of cash. Because the definition of what is considered a cash equivalent is important for preparing an organization's statement of cash flows (which will be discussed in Chapter 3), the rules for determining what can be considered a cash equivalent are set by FASB Statement No. 95, "Statement of Cash Flows" (FAS 95). These requirements define cash equivalents as short-term, highly liquid investments that are both readily convertible to known amounts of cash and so near their maturity that they present an insignificant risk of changes in value because of changes in interest rates. This is interpreted by SFAS 95 to mean that for an investment to be considered a cash equivalent, it must mature within three months of being bought by the organization. This means that a one-year treasury note that is purchased by a not-for-profit organization two months before it matures can be considered a cash equivalent. However, if the not-for-profit purchased the one-year treasury note when it was first issued (so that it matured in one year), it would not be considered a cash equivalent. Also, this investment would not be considered a cash equivalent if it was held by the organization and then reached a point where it only had three months left to maturity. Classification as a cash equivalent occurs when the investment is acquired by the not-for-profit organization. Examples of cash equivalents include Treasury bills, money market funds, and commercial paper. Note again that the term original maturity refers to the length of time to maturity at the time that the security is purchased by the not-for-profit organization, *not* to the security's original duration before maturity.

Investments

An entire chapter of this book (Chapter 5) discusses the accounting for investments by not-for-profit organizations, so not much space will be spent here discussing investments. Suffice it to say that most investments (stocks, bonds, and other debt instruments) are reported in the statement of financial position at their fair value (fair market value is an older term for what is now referred to as fair value). Changes in the fair value of investments from year to year are reported in the not-for-profit organization's statement of activities as part of overall investment earnings (or losses).

Contributions Receivable

Receivables represent money that is owed to the not-for-profit organization. Money may be receivable from any number of sources, but for a not-for-profit organization, most receivables will be from donors or contributors. Donors and contributors may owe the not-for-profit organization contributions that they pledged or promised to give the organization. An entire chapter of this book (Chapter 3) discusses the accounting for these contributions receivable.

Accounts Receivable

The other significant category of receivables, accounts receivable, is often referred to as trade accounts receivable. These receivables represent funds that are owed to the not-for-profit organization from individuals or other organizations because of services provided or goods sold to these other entities. Some common scenarios where these types of receivables may be present on a not-for-profit organization's financial statements are:

- A not-for-profit day-care center may provide services to a local government for children whose day-care the government is paying for. Once the services are provided, the not-for-profit organization has a receivable from the local government until it is paid for those services.

- A not-for-profit college may be owed tuition and fees from students that are past their due date, but have not as yet been paid.
- A not-for-profit club may bill its members for meals and other services that have been provided to the members and are due but have not as yet been paid.

These types of receivables occur from exchange transactions—the not-for-profit organization is not just collecting a donation, it is providing specific services in exchange for money. These business-type activities are becoming an increasingly significant portion of the activities of not-for-profit organizations, because the profit from these activities provides funding for the not-for-profit organization's other activities.

There are two basic considerations that the non-accountant should understand about accounts receivable. First, a receivable (and the related revenue) should not be recorded until the organization actually "earns" the revenue and the right to receive the money from the entity to whom they are selling services. Second, not all receivables are ultimately collected.

Practical Example   Using the day-care services as an example, let us say that a not-for-profit organization wins a contract with a local government to provide day-care services to children referred to it by the local government. The contract is for one year and is of an amount not to exceed $100,000. The local government pays the not-for-profit $50 per day per child that is placed in its care. Some might think that the not-for-profit organization should set up a receivable of $100,000 on its statement of financial position on the date the contract is signed. That is the amount expected to be received under the contract. This is not correct, however, under GAAP. A receivable is only recorded when it, and the related revenue, are earned, which, in this case, is when the day-care center actually cares for a child. In other words, at the end of a week or a month, when the day-care center bills the local government for the services actually provided (number of children for the period times the number of days times $50), that is the time that a receivable should be recorded on the day-care center's books. Obviously, when the local government pays the bill, the receivable is reduced and the increase in cash is recorded on the statement of financial position.

Revenue recognition in the above example is straightforward and thus easy to understand. When transactions are more complex, the determination as to when revenue should be recorded becomes more complicated.

Practical Example   Let us say that a customer of a museum's gift shop purchases a piece of jewelry on June 30, the fiscal year-end of the museum and the gift shop. The customer has an account with the gift shop and will be billed for the purchase. The customer has 10 days to return the item for a complete refund. Will the gift shop record the sale on June 30 (in the current fiscal year) or wait until 10 days have passed and it is certain that the customer will keep the jewelry? *The museum gift shop will record the sale (and the receivable) on June 30.* However, if returns of merchandise are for more than negligible amounts, the museum will likely record an allowance for returns, which will reduce the overall sales and receivable balances for estimated returns.

This example leads into a discussion of the second key point to understand about the accounting for accounts receivable, which is that not all receivables are necessarily collected. GAAP require that an estimate of accounts receivable that will *not* be collected be made and an "allowance for uncollectible accounts receivable" be established. This account reduces the overall receivable balance (and charges bad debt expense), so that the net of the gross receivable balance and the allowance represents the best estimate of how much of the receivable balance actually will be collected. Receivables are therefore reported at their net realizable value, which is in accordance with GAAP. Note that the not-for-profit organization does not really know which receivables it will not collect, but uses historical trends and an aging of its receivable balance (which categorizes how long receivables have been outstanding) to estimate this amount. If the not-for-profit knows that a particular account receivable will not be collected, that particular receivable should be reduced from the gross receivable balance, which is another way of saying that the particular receivable should be written-off.

Other Receivables

Not-for-profit organizations sometimes have other receivables reported on their statement of financial position representing money owed to them for reasons other than the two main categories previously described. The same principles discussed earlier would also apply to these receivables, meaning that they should only be recorded if the organization has a valid claim to them and that they should be reported at a value that represents the amount the organization expects to collect. Some of the common types of these other receivables are:

- *Amounts owed under grants* (the type of grant where no specific action is required by the not-for-profit organization to earn the right to receive the money).
- *Reimbursements of expenses* (for example, a dinner chair agrees to underwrite the costs of a fund-raising dinner).
- *Reimbursement of expenses paid on behalf of other not-for-profit organizations.*

These are only examples—the "other" category can include a wide variety of receivables. If a particular receivable is significant, it should be included as a separate line on the statement of financial position. Alternatively, the details of the "other" category could be described in the notes to the financial statements if the financial statement preparer feels that aggregating too many receivables in the "other" category obscures their nature.

Inventories

Inventories are most often associated with manufacturing and retail operations, rather than not-for-profit organizations. Many not-for-profit organizations *do* maintain inventories, however. Sometimes not-for-profit organizations set up for-profit subsidiaries to handle merchandising activities. This distinction is done basically for tax purposes. A reader of the not-for-profit organization's financial statements will see inventories on the parent not-for-profit organization's statement of financial position when the for-profit subsidiary is consolidated, that is, combined with, the parent organization's financial statements.

Inventories are items that the organization expects to sell. In other words, supplies that are expected to be used by the not-for-profit organization in its operations should not be reported as inventories.

Practical Example   Sometimes there is confusion over these non-inventory items since supplies may be "inventoried" at the end of the fiscal year. If the supplies balance is significant, it should be reported as an asset on the statement of financial position. It should not be included with inventory, which should only represent merchandise held for sale.

Not-for-profit organizations often have inventories of merchandise that they sell, which should be reported as an asset on the statement of financial position. Some common examples of organizations that have inventories are:

- Gift shops of museums, galleries, and other attractions
- Bookstores of not-for-profit colleges and universities
- Snack bars, refreshment stands, or restaurants operated by various types of organizations
- Professional associations, soccer clubs, and other sports clubs that have T-shirts, coffee mugs, and other promotional items held for sale.

The accounting for inventories can be fairly complicated and the details are beyond the scope of this book. In fact, most not-for-profit organizations' merchandising activities are incidental to their overall operations. Hence, a basic understanding of inventory accounting will go a long way in understanding inventories reported on the statement of financial position of a not-for-profit organization.

Inventories are reported on the statement of financial position either at cost or at market value, whichever is lowest. One important matter in accounting for inventories is referred to as the flow assumption. The flow assumption determines which items from inventory are considered to be sold first. The first-in, first-out (FIFO) flow assumption sounds complicated, but simply means that the oldest items from inventory (that is, the first items "in") are the first items to be sold. This is the most common flow assumption used by not-for-profit organizations. Assuming that there is consistent inflation at some level, these older inventory items will have a lower cost assigned to them, because they were theoretically purchased at a lower cost. This means that when these items are sold, the profit realized by the not-for-profit organization will be higher than when the last items brought into inventory are sold. The alternative flow assumption, last-in, first-out (LIFO), assumes that the last items brought into inventory (that is, assuming inflation, the ones with a higher cost) are the first ones sold. This means that when these items are sold, the net profit to the not-for-profit organization is lower than it would be using the FIFO flow assumption. While the LIFO method has clear tax advantages to commercial organizations because reported profits are lower, its use by not-for-profit organizations is less popular, because tax considerations are generally not of paramount importance.

The second important consideration for inventory valuation in the statement of financial position is that the amount reported as the cost of inventories on the statement should not be more than the amount that the inventory can be sold for. The commonly used phrase that inventory is reported at the "lower of cost or market" means just that, with the term market referring to how much the item could be sold for, rather than what it would cost the not-for-profit organization to replace the inventory item.

Red Flag   There are many other inventory methods with intimidating names that are variations on these two basic concepts, such as the *dollar value retail LIFO method*. Particularly when inventory amounts are not significant, not-for-profit organizations sometimes use the average cost of items in inventory to represent the cost of items sold. This results in a sort of hybrid method, combining the features of the FIFO and LIFO methods. While the calculations may grow in complexity, the basic concepts remain as described above.

Property, Plant, and Equipment

Sometimes referred to as fixed assets, the property, plant, and equipment of a not-for-profit organization represent its long-lived assets used in the conduct of the organization's business. These would include land, buildings, equipment, office furnishings, computers, vehicles, and other similar assets. What gets recorded as a capital asset is generally determined by a not-for-profit organization's capitalization policy. This policy determines what purchases are recorded as assets and what purchases are recorded as expenses. If a purchase of one of these types of assets meets the capitalization policy's criteria, it is recorded as an asset. The capitalization policy is usually based on the useful life of the item. Normally, a minimum useful life of three to five years is required before an item is recorded as an asset. The capitalization policy usually also sets a minimum dollar threshold in order for an item to be recorded as an asset. The threshold amount varies based on the size the organization. A $500 threshold is reasonably popular among average-size organizations, although amounts as low as $100 and as high as $10,000 are not uncommon for very small and very large organizations, respectively.

Two other items should be included in fixed assets—leasehold improvements and capitalized leases. Leasehold improvements are purchases that meet the capitalization criteria of an organization, but are improvements to leased property rather than to property owned by the not-for-profit organization itself.

Practical Example A not-for-profit organization enters into a 20-year lease for office space. Prior to moving into the space, the not-for-profit organization "builds out" the space by moving walls to create the desired office space, installing a reception area, carpeting, and so forth. These leasehold improvements would be considered part of the organization's fixed assets although the not-for-profit organization does not own the building to which these improvements are permanently attached.

Capitalized leases (which will be discussed in greater detail in Chapter 10) are an accounting creation that recognizes the substance of some lease transactions over their form. In other words, when a not-for-profit organization enters into a lease for an item, which, in substance, is a purchase of the item, the item is recorded as a fixed asset of the not-for-profit organization, even though the organization does not have title to the asset.

Practical Example A not-for-profit organization leases a copier machine that has a useful life of 10 years. The term of the lease is 10 years. Since the not-for-profit organization is using the asset for virtually its entire useful life, GAAP would require the not-for-profit organization to record the copier as a fixed asset, along with the liability for future lease payments. (These items will also be discussed in Chapter 10 of this book.)

Property, plant, and equipment is recorded on the statement of financial position at its cost to the not-for-profit organization, reduced by accumulated depreciation. Accumulated depreciation represents the decline in value of fixed assets as they are used in the operation of the not-for-profit organization's business. Depreciation expense is the annual amount charged to expense in a not-for-profit organization's statement of activities, which represents an estimate of the amount of the asset that is "used up" in the organization's operations during the year. Accumulated depreciation sums up the annual amounts of depreciation expense for fixed assets and represents a reduction in the recorded cost amount of the asset on the organization's statement of financial position.

Practical Example   A not-for-profit organization buys a PC for $2,200, which it estimates to have a five-year useful life. At the end of five years, the organization expects that it can sell the PC for salvage for $200. The amount to depreciate is $2,000 ($2,200 less the $200 salvage value). $2000 divided by five years results in a depreciation expense of $400 per year. This table illustrates the calculations for the life of this asset:

Year	Depreciation Expense	Accumulated Depreciation	Remaining Net Book Value
1	$400	$400	$1,800
2	$400	$800	$1,400
3	$400	$1,200	$1,000
4	$400	$1,600	$600
5	$400	$2,000	$200

At the end of Year 5, the remaining net book value of the asset ($2,200 original cost less $2,000 accumulated depreciation) equals the estimated salvage value of the asset, $200. No further depreciation would be taken and the asset would remain on the books until it was actually disposed of. If the organization managed to sell the asset for $300, it would remove $2,200 from the asset account and $2,000 from the accumulated depreciation account from the books and record a gain of $100 on the disposition of the asset. If the asset was sold for $100, the organization would remove $2,200 from the asset account and $2,000 from the

accumulated depreciation account from the books and record a
loss of $100 on the disposition of the asset.

Accumulated depreciation is a *contra account* to property, plant,
and equipment, meaning that its balance (which is a credit) off-
sets the gross amount of property, plant, and equipment that is
recorded on the statement of financial position as an asset (debit).
The accumulated depreciation account, as its name suggests, is the
cumulative amount of depreciation that has been recorded on the
assets that are included in property, plant, and equipment. Each
year when depreciation expense is recorded, the accumulated
depreciation amount is increased for the amount of the annual
depreciation expense. Conversely, when an asset is retired or sold,
the amount of accumulated depreciation that is applicable to that
particular asset is removed from accumulated depreciation, meaning that the accumulated depreciation account is reduced for this
amount.

One other relatively new, fancy accounting term related to
property, plant, and equipment may have some applicability to not-
for-profit organizations. This term is *asset impairment.* The accounting rules for asset impairments are found in FASB Statement No.
121, "Accounting for the Impairment of Long-Lived Assets and for
Long-Lived Assets to Be Disposed Of" (FAS 121). Impairment of
long-lived assets occurs when the future benefits (meaning cash
flows) from those assets are less than the net book value of the
asset recorded on an organization's statement of financial position,
or balance sheet. This standard applies more to private-sector accounting and can be explained with a simple example. Let us say
that a manufacturing company owns a plant that produces $5\frac{1}{4}$-
inch floppy disks for personal computers. Sales are understandably down. In fact, sales are only expected to be $5 million in total
for the next five years, at which time the plant can be sold for $10
million. The net book value of the plant on this company's books
is $50 million; it currently has a fair market value of $25 million.
The total expected cash flows from the plant are $15 million ($5
million in sales plus the estimated selling price at the end of the

five years of $10 million). Since $15 million is less than the book value of $50 million, an impairment has occurred. This company measures the amount of the impairment at $25 million, which is the difference between the book value of $50 million and the current fair market value of $25 million. The asset would be reduced to $25 million and a loss would be recognized of $25 million in the period in which the impairment became known as a result of the cash flow test described earlier.

The rules for identifying and recording asset impairment will not directly apply to many not-for-profit organizations, since many of these organizations' assets are not acquired to generate future cash flows. However, not-for-profit organizations that have many business-type activities (for example, colleges and universities and health-care facilities) must be cognizant of the requirements of this accounting principle.

Prepaid Expenses

Prepaid expenses are assets that arise because an organization has paid for services that it will receive in the future, with the future being defined as a time past the fiscal year-end. The most common example of a prepaid expense is an insurance premium. Let us say that a not-for-profit organization has a June 30 fiscal year-end. It pays its general liability insurance premium (assume it is $1,000) on January 1 for the next full calendar year. By June 30, it has used up six months of insurance, but still has another six months of insurance to which it is entitled. This organization would allocate the $1,000 of insurance premium over the 12-month calendar year period. On June 30, it would record a reduction of its insurance expense and record a prepaid insurance expense asset of $500 ($1,000 times 6/12). Note that this organization uses up this prepaid asset during the period from July 1 through December 31. If the organization issued its 6-month financial statements on December 31, it would reduce the entire prepaid asset to zero and record the corresponding $500 as insurance expense, which makes sense because, since the insurance works on a calendar year basis, on December 31, the organization has not prepaid any of its insurance. Assuming in this example that the insurance premiums stay the same every year, the not-for-profit would have recorded $1,000 of insurance expense in its fiscal year ($500 recognized as a result of the premium payment and $500 recognized when the prepaid expense asset is used up).

While prepaid insurance is the most common and easily understood example of a prepaid expense, there can be many others. Rental payments on facilities or equipment are another example. Some judgment should be used by not-for-profit organizations in determining what should be recorded as prepaid expenses. For example, a motor vehicle registration fee is usually paid annually in advance. If the not-for-profit organization only owns a few motor vehicles, it is probably not worth the administrative effort to calculate and record this type of prepaid expense, particularly when registrations expire throughout the year.

Liabilities

FASB Concepts Statement No. 6 provides this definition of liabilities: "Liabilities are probable future sacrifices of economic benefits arising from present obligations of a particular entity to transfer assets or provide services to other entities in the future as a result of past transactions or events." While this definition is somewhat less confusing than FASB Concepts Statement No. 6's definition of assets, it still requires a good deal of explanation. Non-accountants generally think of liabilities as simply "money that you owe." While this is not too far off from a GAAP perspective, there are several ideas in Statement 6's definition that will make the simple definition more accurate.

First, liabilities are measured at a point in time, which means, for financial statement purposes, as of the end of the not-for-profit organization's fiscal year. To be a present obligation means that the obligation has actually been incurred as of the year-end to be reported on the statement of financial position as a liability, meaning it is the result of past transactions or events. Second, the obligations are not simply those that must be satisfied by the payment of cash. Liabilities also consist of obligations of the not-for-profit organization to perform services or transfer assets other than cash to the party to which the organization is obligated.

Some of the more common liabilities found recorded on the statement of financial position of not-for-profit organizations are:

- Accounts payable and accrued expenses
- Debt
- Deferred income

Sometimes not-for-profit organizations report both accounts payable and accrued expenses on one line on the statement of financial position. Other times, separate amounts are reported for each. For the purpose of explaining what these liabilities represent, it is helpful to discuss accounts payable and accrued expenses together.

Accounts payable essentially represent the unpaid bills of a not-for-profit organization. These are bills for goods or services that have been received by the organization prior to the end of its fiscal year.

Practical Example   The not-for-profit organization receives an invoice in the amount of $1000 for stationery that it ordered for a fund-raising campaign. The stationery was received on June 15. The fiscal year-end of the organization is June 30, and a check for $1,000 was issued to the stationery supply store on July 7. As of June 30, the not-for-profit organization records a $1,000 accounts payable (representing the unpaid invoice) along with a $1,000 supplies expense. (Note that accounts payable also arise when a not-for-profit organization buys assets or incurs expenses.)

There are two other situations that might also give a not-for-profit organization cause to record amounts as accounts payable, and both of these situations involve issuance of checks. Let us say that a not-for-profit organization with a June 30 year-end writes checks for all of its outstanding bills on June 29, even though it realizes that it will not have available funds in its bank account to clear the checks until the second week of July. The not-for-profit organization holds all of the checks written on June 29 and first mails them on July 12. When the checks are written, most automated (and manual) accounting systems would record a decrease in cash and a decrease in accounts payable. However, in this example, the not-for-profit organization has neither expended cash nor reduced its accounts payable on June 30—all it really did was write checks. Accordingly, the total amount of the checks held by the not-for-profit organization until past year-end would be added back to cash and to accounts payable.

A second similar situation arises when the not-for-profit organization writes checks prior to its year-end and reduces the book balance of its cash below zero. It can do this because it knows that all of the written checks will take some time to clear the bank, at which time the not-for-profit organization expects that the actual balance in its bank account—its bank balance—will be sufficient to clear the checks. The difference between this case and the first situation is that, in this case, the not-for-profit organization does not physically hold onto the checks. It mails them. In this case, the not-for-profit organization would not report a negative balance for cash on its statement of financial position. Rather, it would bring the book balance of the account up to zero and would add the same amount to its accounts payable balance. Effectively, this reclassifies the negative book balance of cash to accounts payable.

Accrued expenses represent liabilities for goods and services received by a not-for-profit organization for which either an invoice has not been received or the entire invoice does not apply to the fiscal year-end being reported. A simple example should make this clear:

Practical Example   Referring to the $1,000 stationery purchase example used above, let us say that the not-for-profit organization did *not* receive the invoice for the stationery until July 7. Assuming that the physical delivery of the stationery still occurred on or before June 30, the organization would record an accrued expense for this purchase. Basically, a liability is recorded for the accrued expenses and, at the same time, stationery expense is charged. Also keep in mind that amounts might have to be estimated for shipping or similar charges in establishing the accrued expense. Conversely, the not-for-profit organization may take into consideration discounts for prompt payment that it intends to take, if it is the organization's normal practice to take advantage of such discounts.

Accrued expenses also arise because invoice amounts or service periods span the end of the fiscal year of an organization. For example, if a monthly telephone bill covers a period that ends on the 15th of each month, the organization should accrue a telephone expense for that portion of the July 15 telephone bill that applies to the fiscal year ending on June 30, which would be for the period from June 16 (first day of the bill period) through June 30.

A similar accrued expense concept applies to salary expenses where the pay period does not coincide with the end of a fiscal year. Only the portion of the weekly or biweekly salary expense (including related fringe benefit expenses) that is earned by employees up to and including the date of the fiscal year-end should be accrued as salary (and fringe benefit) expense through the end of the organization's fiscal year-end.

Debt

In addition to the accounts payable and accrued expense liabilities described above, not-for-profit organizations generally have a iiability for at least some form of debt which they have incurred. Debt is known by several different names, usually based on how long the debt has before it becomes due, or matures. For example, a short-term loan is generally evidenced by some type of legal instrument, commonly referred to as a note. These types of loans are usually recorded in the financial statements as notes payable, and generally mature in five years or less. There are a wide variety of transactions that may give rise to notes payable, some of which are very common. For example, a not-for-profit organization may purchase new office equipment and desire to pay off the purchase price over a three-year period. The equipment seller would usually have the organization sign a promissory note for the purchase price, providing a legal basis for their future right to collect the purchase price, including interest, from the not-for-profit organization.

Another common form of short-term debt incurred by not-for-profit organizations is that of short-term cash advances received from lines of credit. Often, not-for-profit organizations receive donations on a cyclical basis. December is a popular time for donations, as the holiday season puts many donors in the spirit to give and donors rush to make contributions before the end of the calendar year for tax purposes. However, since a not-for-profit organization's cash needs may be quite different from its pattern of cash receipts, many organizations obtain a credit line from a bank to help them through any cash-short times. It is important to note that a liability is *not* recorded at the time that the not-for-profit organization obtains the line of credit, but rather when it draws down on the credit line. For example, assume that the organization negotiates with a bank and obtains a credit line of $10,000. No money is borrowed, but similar to a consumer home equity credit line, the $10,000 is available at will by the not-for-profit organization. No liability is recorded at this time, although the existence of the credit line must be disclosed in the notes to the financial statements. Let us say that during the year the not-for-profit organization draws $8,000 against the line, and at the end of the fiscal year the $8,000 is still outstanding. The statement of financial position would show a liability of $8,000 (in addition to any amount of accrued interest expense that should be recorded), reflecting the actual amount owed under the credit line.

Longer-term debt incurred by a not-for-profit organization is usually associated with the construction of a facility or other major capital improvement. Long-term debt may take the form of bonds or a mortgage or other long-term financing from a financial institution.

Larger not-for-profit organizations sometimes issue bonds to finance construction or purchase of significant facilities. The specific mechanics of these types of transactions are beyond the scope of this book. Suffice it to say that the unpaid principal of the bonds will be recorded as a liability on the statement of financial position of the not-for-profit organization. Since bonds can be sold at either a discount (e.g., a $1,000 face value bond can only be initially sold for $980) or a premium (e.g., a $1,000 face value bond is initially sold for $1,020), the liability recorded on the financial statements would represent the face amount of the bonds (also called their par value), decreased by discounts and increased on premiums on the initial sales of the bonds. Note that the total of the discounts or premiums is amortized (reduced) over the life of the bond. This amortization results in either a decrease in interest expense (in the case of a discount) or an increase in interest expense (in the case of a premium).

Other long-term financing obtained by a not-for-profit organization often takes the form of bank loans secured by mortgages against the specific facilities constructed. The outstanding balances of these loans are reported as liabilities on the statement of financial position of the not-for-profit organization.

All types of debt incurred by not-for-profit organizations will give rise to interest expense. Interest expense follows similar concepts for accruing other types of expenses. Interest expense is recognized as an expense when it is earned by the holder of the not-for-profit organization's debt, regardless of when the interest is actually paid, as explained in this example:

Practical Example   A not-for-profit organization with a September 30 year-end makes semiannual interest payments—on January 1 and July 1 each year—on bonds that is has sold. Interest is paid in arrears, which means that it is paid after it has been earned by the bond holder. In other words, the January 1 interest payment is for interest earned by the bond holder from July 1 to December 31. Accordingly, the January 1 interest payment includes interest relating to the period of July 1 through September 30. Interest related to this period must be accrued by the not-for-profit organization in its September 30 financial statements. Accruing interest results in the recording of an accrued interest liability (another type of accrued expense liability as previously discussed), with a corresponding amount recorded as interest expense. When the actual payment is made on January 1, the accrued interest liability is reduced to zero, with the balance of the interest payment recognized as interest expense in the year that the payment is made.

Deferred Income

The liabilities discussed in the preceding pages are relatively easy to understand. However, liability for deferred income requires a little more conceptual thinking to understand. The idea of recording deferred income is matching the recording of income with the period in which the revenue is earned, which in some cases also matches the revenue to the costs incurred to generate that revenue. When cash is received by a not-for-profit organization prior to its either having earned the income or the right to keep the income, it records the cash along with a liability-type account called deferred income. Two examples should make this clearer:

Practical Example   A performing arts organization sells subscriptions of tickets to its events for the year. One event is held each month beginning in January. A season's subscription (12 events) must be paid for in advance, prior to January. This organization earns its subscription revenue as the monthly events are performed. In the December prior to the start of the season, it would record all cash it received for subscriptions to the upcoming season as deferred revenue. As each event is performed, it earns $1/12$ of its subscription revenue. Accordingly, each month following the event, deferred income would be reduced by $1/12$ of the original amount recorded and event income would be recorded for the corresponding amount. At the end of the season after all events have been performed, all subscription revenue would be earned, meaning that deferred income would have been reduced to zero and the entire proceeds of the subscriptions would have been recorded as revenue. This accounting technique matches the revenue recognized to the accounting period in which the event was performed that generated, or earned, that revenue. It also matches, at least partially, the recognition of revenue to the costs of production that are incurred by the performing arts organization relating to the performance.

Practical Example   As will be discussed in much greater detail later in this book, donors may make contributions to not-for-profit organizations that are conditional. Stretching the above example a little, let us say that a patron makes a $5,000 contribution to the organization in December 2001 and stipulates in a letter accompanying the check that unless the performing arts organization stages the donor's favorite concert in July 2002, the organization must return the contribution. The organization's right to keep the $5,000 doesn't become unconditional until the donor's favorite concert is performed in July 2002. The organization would record the initial receipt of the check in December 2001 as deferred income. After the required concert is performed in July 2002, the contribution becomes unconditional. The organization would reduce the deferred income related to this contribution to zero and record a corresponding amount of contribution revenue.

Net Assets

The difference between the assets and liabilities of a not-for-profit organization is its net assets. Net assets are a not-for-profit organization's equivalent of stockholder's equity in the commercial world or fund balance in the governmental accounting world. While the total of net assets is simple to calculate (assets less liabilities), what makes net assets somewhat difficult to understand is that when preparing financial statements in accordance with GAAP, net assets must be split into three different classifications:

- Unrestricted net assets
- Temporarily restricted net assets
- Permanently restricted net assets

Important note: While only net assets need be displayed in these three categories, the not-for-profit organization must be able to identify the assets and liabilities that would fall within each of the three classifications, as well as the additions and deductions from each of the three classifications. Remember that net assets are the result of a calculation (assets less liabilities), so that to classify net assets, the financial statement preparer needs to know what assets and liabilities fall into each of these classifications. In practice, this is not as difficult to do as it may appear. Usually the organization knows its temporarily and permanently restricted assets fairly well, and then assumes everything else is unrestricted.

Unrestricted Net Assets

Unrestricted net assets represent the net assets of a not-for-profit organization that are not temporarily restricted or permanently restricted. As will be explained in the following sections, the *temporary* and *permanent* restrictions that result in those two classifications of net assets are the results of restrictions made by donors. In the absence of a donor restriction, assets and liabilities are unrestricted and the difference between the two is reported as unrestricted net assets.

Some not-for-profit organizations have assets that are designated by their boards of directors to be held for specific purposes. For example, to provide a financial cushion and to generate investment income, a board of directors may designate that the organization set aside some level of assets in a "board-designated investment fund." Similarly, boards of directors might designate certain amounts of net assets that are being held and accumulated over a period of years for a major construction project. These board of directors' designations are *not* donor restrictions, and net assets relating to them are reported as unrestricted net assets.

Similarly, some not-for-profit organizations may view all of their net assets as restricted because all of the assets of the organization must be used for purposes of fulfilling the organization's exempt purpose, as set out in its charter, bylaws, tax-exemption designation, and so on. While it is true that the net assets of a not-for-profit organization that runs a homeless shelter are restricted in that it cannot simply take its assets and build a casino, this is not a specific donor restriction that would result in assets being classified as anything but unrestricted. The same goes for the argument "Well, although our donors made general contributions to our organization, they clearly gave us money to run a homeless shelter, not to build a casino. Therefore, these net assets are restricted." This is not correct, because there are no specific restrictions from a donor related to specific contributions. These are general contributions that are not restricted by the donors in any way other than the nature of the organization, its articles of incorporation, bylaws, and so forth.

Temporarily Restricted Net Assets

Temporarily restricted net assets are those net assets whose use is limited by either a donor-imposed time restriction or a donor-imposed purpose restriction. A time restriction requires that the net assets be used during a certain period of time. Sometimes time restrictions specify that the net assets cannot be used until after a specific point in time. A purpose restriction, as its name suggests, requires that resources be used for a specific purpose, such as a specific program of the organization. Examples will help clarify these concepts:

Practical Example   A donor makes a $5,000 contribution to a school in May 2002 and specifies that the money be used by the school for the next school year, which begins in September 2002. This is a time restriction, and the $5,000 in cash would be considered an addition to temporarily restricted net assets until the time restriction was met, which would be when the new school year begins. Note that the $5,000 is recorded as contribution revenue when it is received as an increase in temporarily restricted net assets. Once the school year begins, the school is free to spend the money as it sees fit, so the $5,000 of assets is reclassified, that is, moved, to unrestricted net assets.

The reader is strongly encouraged to refer back to the discussion of deferred income in the prior section in which a donor condition resulted in a contribution being recorded as deferred income, that is, *not* contribution revenue, because the organization had to do something in the future to earn the right to keep the money. When a contribution is recorded as deferred income, there is no effect on net assets because an asset is being recorded (cash) as well as a liability (deferred income). Since net assets equal assets less liabilities and both assets and liabilities were increased by the same amount, there is no impact on net assets. In the school example, the school does not have to do anything to keep the money, it simply has to wait until September to spend it. This is a donor *restriction* which is different from the donor *condition* of the performing arts organization. Additional discussions of contributions can be found in Chapter 3 of this book.

Practical Example   A donor purpose restriction can arise when a not-for-profit organization has several programs that it administers and donors would like to restrict the use of their contributions to a specific program. Referring to the school example above, let us assume that the donor does not specify when the $5,000 contribution must be spent, but instead specifies that the $5,000 be used to create a new art studio for the school. The donor has restricted the purpose for which the funds can be spent. Until the $5,000 is spent on a new art studio, it would be reported as part of temporarily restricted net assets. When the expenses are incurred in setting up the new art studio and the $5,000 is spent, an accounting entry is recorded in which the $5,000 is reclassified to unrestricted net assets so that it offsets the expenses of setting up the art studio, which are first paid out of unrestricted net assets. Note that expenses are paid from the not-for-profit organization's unrestricted net assets. Unrestricted net assets are "reimbursed" by re-classifying assets from temporarily restricted net assets to unrestricted net assets. Temporarily restricted net assets, accordingly, are then reduced to zero, which makes sense, because the funds have been spent on their restricted purpose.

Permanently Restricted Net Assets

As the name implies, permanently restricted net assets represent those net assets that a donor has instructed the not-for-profit organization to maintain in perpetuity, that is, permanently. The most common type of permanently restricted net asset arises from an endowment received by a not-for-profit organization. In the most common form of this type of transaction, a donor contributes assets (cash or investments) to a not-for-profit organization with the instructions that the corpus of the endowment fund not be spent, but that the organization can use the income generated by the endowment fund in conjunction with its activities. The income may be considered temporarily restricted or unrestricted, depending on the terms of the endowment agreement. In addition, appreciation in the value of investments made under an endowment agreement may be permanently restricted either by the donor or as a result of applicable state law. More information on donor restrictions on contributed assets is provided in Chapter 3.

Revenues

FASBCS 6 defines revenues as "inflows or other enhancements of assets of an entity or settlement of its liabilities (or a combination of both) from delivering or producing goods, receiving services, or other activities that constitute the entity's ongoing major or central operations." Not-for-profit organizations usually refer to donations as "support" and include support amount with other revenues that the organizations earn. This terminology acknowledges that contributions do not fit nicely into the true definition of a revenue, but are usually not-for-profit organizations' principal source of resources and should be treated as revenues. In most cases, not-for-profit organizations receive revenues in the form of cash. Sometimes revenue may initially be recorded as a receivable if the revenue is not received in cash when the not-for-profit organization has earned the revenue and has a legal right to its collection. Keep in mind that under this definition, donated goods and services are also considered revenue (or "support and revenue," in not-for-profit terminology). Similarly, if a donor or other party satisfies an outstanding liability of the not-for-profit organization, the organization would also record revenue, or support and revenue.

Not-for-profit organizations generally have two primary sources of revenues: contributions (sometimes called "support and contributions") and fee-for-service activities. Contributions are addressed in much more detail in Chapter 3 of this book. For the purpose of understanding contributions in the context of all of the revenues of a not-for-profit organization, it is sufficient to say that contribution revenues are recognized and recorded in the financial statements of a not-for-profit organization when the organization has an unconditional right to receive those revenues.

Accounting for fee-for-service revenues of a not-for-profit organization closely resembles the accounting for revenues by commercial organizations under GAAP. As briefly described earlier in this chapter, fee-for-service activities of a not-for-profit organization represent those activities where there is a direct exchange of value between the not-for-profit organization and the individual or entity purchasing the goods or services. Here are some examples of fee-for-service activities commonly found at not-for-profit organizations:

- A college or university provides education for a tuition payment.
- A visitor to a zoo buys a toy stuffed animal at the zoo's gift shop.
- A professional organization provides services to its members in return for annual membership dues.

- A day-care center provides a certain number of days of day-care to an agreed-on number of children under a contract with a local government.
- Parents buy a hot dog and soda from an athletic association's snack bar at their child's soccer tournament.

Fee-for-service revenues are recognized (i.e., reported as revenues in their financial statements) when the service is provided. This is easy to identify in the simple transactions described above. The cash collected for the hot dog and soda is recognized at the time of the purchase. For the day-care contract with a local government, the fee is most likely earned by the day-care center when it provides the service to the children in its care. Accordingly, revenue is recognized as the day-care center performs its services and bills the local government. Revenue is not recognized at the time that this type of contract is signed, which is a frequent misconception among readers of not-for-profit organization financial statements. As described earlier in this chapter, if the day-care center received a cash advance from the government at the time that the contract was signed or at the beginning of the service period, the day-care center would record the cash advance as deferred income recognized. Revenue would be recognized (and the deferred revenue amount recorded on the statement of financial position reduced) as the services were performed by the day-care center.

Expenses

FASBCS-6 defines expenses as ". . . outflows or other using up of assets or incurrence of liabilities (or a combination of both) from delivering or producing goods, rendering services, or carrying out other activities that constitute the entity's ongoing major or central operations." This definition is similar in format to that of revenues, except that expenses refer to the using up of resources while revenues refer to obtaining resources. Expense recognition was discussed briefly earlier in this chapter with regard to accounts payable and accrued expenses. Worth noting in this discussion, however, is that the above definition refers to a using up of assets, which does not always mean a payment in cash. For example, some of the assets described earlier in this chapter (inventory and prepaid expenses, for example) are treated as an asset when the cash is expended (or an accounts payable or accrued expense is recorded). These assets are then charged to expense either when time passes (in the case of prepaid expenses) or as the assets are sold or used by the organization (in the case of inventory). Similarly, property, plant, and equipment is originally recorded as an asset and then depreciated (except for land, which is not depreciated) using some systematic method. The depreciation calculated for each year is recorded as an expense of that period.

As will be discussed in the next chapter on the key financial statements of a not-for-profit organization, there are two important classifications of expenses used by not-for-profit organizations: functional and natural.

Functional Classification

This classification provides an indication of what the expenses were used for by the not-for-profit organization. The three principal functional classifications are:

- *Program expenses.* These are expenses that the not-for-profit organization incurs in the operation of its various program activities.
- *Management and administrative expenses.* These are the expenses incurred by the not-for-profit organization in its overall management and administration that are not identifiable with any particular program. (These expenses are sometimes called general and administrative expenses.)
- *Fund-raising expenses.* These are the expenses incurred by the not-for-profit organization in its efforts to raise money from donors.

Not-for-profit organizations that are membership organizations would report a fourth classification of functional expenses, membership development expenses. These are expenses incurred by the membership organization in soliciting for new members and membership dues.

Natural Classification

This classification indicates the type of expense that was incurred by the not-for-profit organization. Examples of the natural classification of expenses would be salary expenses, rent, electricity, depreciation, and so on.

Whereas functional classification indicates on what activity (function) the not-for-profit organization incurred the expense, natural classification indicates the type (nature) of the expense that was incurred. Each of these classifications will be discussed more fully in Chapter 2 of this book, in the section covering the statement of activities.

Gains and Losses

Revenues of not-for-profit organizations *increase* their net assets; expenses *decrease* net assets. All other transactions that increase or decrease the net assets of a not-for-profit organization are referred to as gains or losses, respectively. (An exception to this broad statement are equity transactions with the "owners" of an organization, such as a capitalization investment or a dividend or other distributions to owners. These are infrequent transactions in not-for-profit organizations.)

What distinguishes gains and losses from revenues and expenses centers on the phrase in both the definition of revenues and of expenses that they are transactions that ". . . constitute the entity's ongoing major or central operations." Gains and losses are transactions that are auxiliary to the not-for-profit organization's revenues and expenses. Investment gains or losses are very common examples of this type of transaction for not-for-profit organizations. Another example would include the gain or loss recorded on the sale of an asset, such as gains or losses resulting from the sale of a building or other fixed asset. In evaluating what transactions would be considered revenues/ expenses or gains/losses, the nature of the operations of the not-for-profit organization needs to be evaluated. A transaction that would be considered outside of one organization's central operations, might be considered part of another organization's central operations and, accordingly, be included in revenues and expenses.

WHAT IS MEANT BY THE ACCRUAL BASIS OF ACCOUNTING? HOW DOES THIS DIFFER FROM THE CASH BASIS OF ACCOUNTING, AND WHICH IS BETTER?

Non-accountants tend to think, understandably so, that there is only one way that organizations record transactions. In other words, they believe the basis of accounting used by any not-for-profit organization should be the same as that used by any other organization. The old joke that an accountant's answer to the question "How much is two plus two?" is *"How much do you want it to be?"* had to have started somewhere, and maybe having more than one accounting basis is the place where it started.

The most important item to keep in mind in distinguishing between the accrual basis of accounting and the cash basis of accounting is that *only* the accrual basis of accounting is acceptable under generally accepted accounting principles. Any auditor's report accompanying financial statements prepared using the cash basis of accounting must include a statement that the financial statements are not prepared in accordance with generally accepted accounting principles. In trying to understand what is really meant by a "basis of accounting," keep in mind that the accounting basis essentially determines when (that is, in which accounting period) a transaction is recorded. We will now describe the principle differences between the accrual and cash bases of accounting in more detail.

Accrual Basis

The discussion of the various assets, liabilities, revenues, and expenses provided earlier in this chapter included the basic principles underlying the accrual basis of accounting. Revenues are recognized when they are earned, regardless of when the cash is actually collected. Revenues must also be realizable, meaning that the organization must at some time in the future be able to convert any receivables resulting from revenue recognition. If the organization does not expect to ever collect the cash from a revenue transaction, it should not record a receivable for it. Under the accrual basis of accounting, not-for-profit organizations record a donor's unconditional promise to give as revenue (and receivable), provided that the contribution is realizable, that is, the not-for-profit organization ultimately expects to collect the contribution.

Expenses recorded on the accrual basis of accounting follow three basic principles:

- *First, some expenses are recognized when they are "matched" to the revenue which they generate.* For example, when an item of inventory is sold, the "expense" for the item sold (basically, the not-for-profit organization's cost) is recognized at the same time as the revenue from the sale is recorded. Accordingly, the revenue and the related cost, or expense, is matched and recognized in the same fiscal year, or other accounting period.
- *Second, some expenses are recognized in the fiscal year or accounting period in which they are used by the organization.* The majority of the management, general expenses, and fund-raising expenses are recorded when the cash is paid or when the liability is incurred by the not-for-profit organization. In other words, these types of expenses are recognized when the organization has an obligation to pay the expense, which will generally correspond with the period in which the organization receives the benefit of the expense. For

example, rent expense should be recognized in the period in which the organization occupies the rented premises. Salary expense is recognized in the period during which the employees perform services. Utility expense is recognized in the period in which the particular service (telephone, electricity, gas, water, etc.) is used or consumed by the not-for-profit organization.

- *Third, some expenses are the result of a systematic allocation of costs to accounting periods.* Depreciation expense related to the depreciation of fixed assets is the classic example of this type of expense.

In considering the accrual basis of accounting, keep in mind that the time of the actual cash receipt or cash disbursement does not determine in which accounting period a transaction is recorded. Rather, revenues and expenses are recorded using the above principles, regardless of when the actual cash is collected or disbursed.

Cash Basis

Under the cash basis of accounting, transactions are only recorded when cash is received or disbursed. The terms revenues and expenses should not be used in the cash basis of accounting. Rather, only the terms *cash receipts* and *cash disbursements* should be used. In a pure application of the cash basis of accounting, the only asset of the organization would be the balance in its cash accounts. There would be no liabilities, and the cash balance would equal the total net assets of the not-for-profit organization. In actual practice, not-for-profit organizations seldom use a pure cash basis of accounting. More often, a modified cash basis is used, in which recognition may be given in the financial statements to certain receivables that are expected to be collected shortly after year-end as well as to certain payables that usually represent the unpaid bills of the organization. In addition, property, plant, and equipment, and long-term debt are also sometimes recorded. Other variations to the pure cash basis of accounting are common and are usually based on the specific needs of the organization.

Accountants almost universally agree that the accrual basis of accounting presents a better picture of an organization's financial position and results of operations and is, therefore, the only acceptable method for financial reporting in accordance with generally accepted accounting principles. The obvious question, then, is: Why would some not-for-profit organizations elect to use the cash or modified cash basis of accounting for preparing financial statements? The answer is that, particularly for small organizations, the cash basis of accounting may meet the basic needs of the users of the financial statements of the not-for-profit organization. Managers and overseers of the activities of the not-for-profit organization may feel more comfortable with the cash basis of accounting because it is generally easier to understand than the accrual basis. (Readers of this book should not fall into this category!) In addition, the cash basis of accounting is much simpler to apply than the accrual basis, meaning that it is more likely that the accounting staff of the not-for-profit organization will be able (or willing) to undertake full responsibility for preparation of the financial statements. Many small organizations that *do* use the accrual basis of accounting rely on their independent auditors to develop the necessary journal entries needed to convert from cash basis accounting records to accrual basis financial statements. This extra work, on top of the additional procedures that an independent auditor generally needs to perform in auditing accrual basis financial statements versus cash basis financial statements, will very likely result in higher audit costs for accrual basis financial statements than cash basis financial statements. The added complexities and costs associated with the accrual basis may induce many smaller not-for-profit organizations to prepare financial statements using the cash basis of accounting.

In considering the use of the cash basis of accounting, several matters should be kept in mind:

- *An independent auditor may issue an opinion that cash basis financial statements are prepared in accordance with the cash basis,*

which would be described in a note to the financial statements.
The auditor's opinion would note, however, that the financial statements are not prepared in accordance with generally accepted accounting principles.

- *Virtually all states have filing requirements for not-for-profit organizations, which usually require submission of financial statements.*
State and other laws or contracts or donor agreements may require the not-for-profit organization to submit financial statements prepared in accordance with generally accepted accounting principles. Again, the cash basis of accounting could not be used in these circumstances.

- *Current and future creditors may not actually demand financial statements prepared in accordance with generally accepted accounting principles, but may feel more secure from a lending perspective if they are able to obtain GAAP statements from the not-for-profit organization.* Again, the accrual basis of accounting would be used.

As a hybrid methodology, many not-for-profit organizations maintain their books during the fiscal year on the cash basis of accounting and then prepare (or have their independent auditors prepare) the necessary adjusting journal entries to convert the cash basis accounting records into accrual basis financial statements. A word of caution in using this approach involves how an organization prepares and adopts an annual budget for its activities. Comparing monthly cash basis statements with an annual accrual basis budget can result in some important inconsistencies, particularly in types of expenses that are never recorded on a cash basis, such as depreciation expense. Adding these additional expenses at year-end may have a dramatic impact in determining whether the organization stayed within its budget during the fiscal year. It can also negate the effectiveness of a monthly or quarterly budget as an effective management tool. Determining how these noncash types of year-end adjusting entries are to be handled should be accomplished at the time that the budget is prepared and adopted, so that there are no year-end surprises for the not-for-profit organization's management and board of directors.

WHAT HAPPENED TO FUND ACCOUNTING?

Some readers of a book on not-for-profit accounting principles might have expected to read a long discussion of the intricacies of fund accounting. If this book were being written ten years ago, this topic would have been one of the first in this chapter, rather than the last. The fact is that, for the purpose of preparing financial statements in accordance with GAAP subsequent to the adoption of SFAS 117, reporting information by funds is no longer required. Fund accounting has essentially been replaced by classifications of net assets into their unrestricted, temporarily restricted, and permanently restricted categories.

Some not-for-profit organizations continue to use fund accounting in their internal accounting systems and then convert this information into net asset classifications for purposes of financial reporting. Since SFAS 117 does not preclude presentation of fund information (as long as its required net asset information is presented), some not-for-profit organizations still present some fund financial information in their financial statements prepared in accordance with GAAP. These organizations might present information about their current funds, which include both restricted and unrestricted amounts, endowment funds, and plant funds (in which they record property, plant, and equipment). Frankly, presentation of fund information in financial statements prepared in accordance with SFAS 117 can make the financial statements confusing, at best, and contradictory, at worst. Unless there is an overriding reason as to why this information is important to particular readers of financial statements, it is probably best to leave it out.

One of the primary reasons for using fund accounting was to improve the accountability of certain not-for-profit organizations that often found themselves in the somewhat unique circumstance of only being able to use some of their assets for certain purposes or programs. Fund accounting assisted in assuring compliance with these requirements. On the other hand, the fairly sophisticated accounting software packages available today can provide a high degree of accountability, assuming that the organization's chart of accounts and cost allocations are set up with some thought and care. As more and more not-for-profit organizations convert to more sophisticated systems, it seems likely that true fund accounting will gradually disappear from use.

The management of each not-for-profit organization should assess whether the use of fund accounting still makes sense for its particular organization. Consultation with the organization's independent auditor prior to abandoning a fund accounting system is encouraged to make sure that any new system or approach to accumulating and reporting information for GAAP financial statements (as well as any donor or grantor requirements for financial information of individual programs or grants) will still accumulate the required information at the necessary level of detail.

SUMMARY

This chapter presented a foundation for a basic level of understanding of the application of generally accepted accounting principles to not-for-profit organizations. The common features of not-for-profit financial statements presented as an overview will serve as a foundation for understanding the finer points of not-for-profit accounting described in subsequent chapters.

CHAPTER 2

Basic Financial Statements of a Not-for-Profit Organization

The purpose of this chapter is to provide the non-accountant with an overall understanding of the content and purpose of each of the financial statements of a not-for-profit organization, which together constitute a complete set of financial statements prepared in accordance with generally accepted accounting principles. The rules for not-for-profit organization financial reporting were established by FASB Statement No. 117, "Financial Statements of Not-for-Profit Organizations" (SFAS 117). Prior to the issuance of SFAS 117, a variety of Accounting and Audit Guides issued by the American Institute of Certified Public Accountants (AICPA) provided basic guidance for the preparation of not-for-profit financial statements. Under these Accounting and Audit Guides, different types of not-for-profit organizations used different accounting and financial reporting practices. Under SFAS 117, almost all of these disparities have been eliminated, resulting in fairly homogeneous financial reporting standards for all types of not-for-profit organizations. This helps the non-accountant understand not-for-profit financial statements because of their similarity and the fact that there is basically one set of standards to follow.

The basic financial statements of a not-for-profit organization include:

- Statement of financial position
- Statement of activities
- Statement of cash flows
- Notes to the financial statements

Each of these statements will be described in more detail in the following sections of this chapter.

STATEMENT OF FINANCIAL POSITION

Many non-accountants would probably refer to the statement of financial position as a balance sheet. The statement of financial position provides a snapshot of a not-for-profit organization's assets, liabilities, and net assets. When presenting a complete set of financial statements in accordance with GAAP, the statement of financial position should be prepared as of the not-for-profit organization's fiscal year-end. (A sample statement of financial position is provided in Exhibit 2.1 on page 5.)

Information about Net Assets and Donor Restrictions

The format of the statement of financial position usually begins with all of the assets of the organization and deducts the liabilities of the organization to arrive at a calculation of net assets. The statement should display separate net asset amounts for the three classifications of net assets (unrestricted, temporarily restricted, and permanently restricted) as well as the total of net assets.

Information is generally included in the statement of financial position about restricted assets. This information is usually provided by using separate line items within the statement to report both temporarily restricted assets and permanently restricted ones. In addition, differences in types of temporary restrictions—time restrictions and purpose restrictions (which will be discussed in Chapter 3)—might also be disclosed on separate line items. Likewise, differences in permanent restrictions might also be dis-

closed on separate line items. For example, a collection of historical treasures donated to a museum with a permanent restriction
that they be held in perpetuity for public exhibition would be reported separately from an endowment fund in which a group of
investments is permanently restricted by a donor to produce an
investment income, which is available for the not-for-profit
organization to use. As an alternative, this information can be disclosed by the not-for-profit organization in the notes to the financial statements. However, it is a good practice to make sure that
the reader of the statement of financial position can readily distinguish between those assets that can be used by the organization
in an unrestricted manner and those that have donor restrictions.
The nature of the restrictions and the extent to which total net
assets are comprised of a significant amount of donor restrictions
is likely to dictate whether information is provided on the face of
the statement or in the notes to the financial statements. If the
extent of asset restrictions is fairly limited and affects only a
few nonliquid assets, disclosure in the notes to the financial statements may be appropriate. On the other hand, if there are significant restrictions to a considerable amount of assets, display of this
information on the face of the statement of financial position is
more appropriate.

Information on Liquidity

Providing information about liquidity is an important concept promulgated by SFAS 117 in presenting the statement of financial
condition. Liquidity of assets means how close assets are to conversion to cash. Information about liquidity provides the financial
statement reader with information that can be used to analyze
whether a not-for-profit organization can currently be expected to
pay its bills. For liabilities, liquidity means the closeness to the
maturity date of the liability. SFAS 117 provides not-for-profit organizations with two options for providing information on liquidity: (1) sequencing assets and liabilities and (2) presenting a classified balance sheet.

Sequencing of Assets and Liabilities

In this method, the not-for-profit organization provides information about liquidity by the order in which assets and liabilities are presented. Assets that are nearest to conversion to cash are presented first, and so on, until the last assets that are presented are those farthest from conversion to cash. For example, an investment is much nearer to conversion to cash than property, plant, and equipment.

Liabilities are presented in the order of their maturity. For example, accounts payable, which are generally due in 30 days, would be listed before a long-term bond, which might first mature in 30 years. (Note that if there is a current portion of the long-term debt due before 30 years' time, this would be shown separately as a liability much nearer to maturity than the remaining long-term portion of the debt.)

Providing Liquidity Information in a Classified Statement of Financial Position

In a classified balance sheet, both assets and liabilities are classified as current and noncurrent. As will be seen in Chapter 11, which discusses financial ratios used to evaluate liquidity, a classified balance sheet makes financial statement analysis a little easier for the financial statement user.

A current asset is one that will be converted to cash or used in the business within one year. Examples include cash, short-term investments, contributions and other receivables, inventories, and prepaid expenses. Current assets would *not* include those assets restricted for use in the operation of the organization, meaning that many assets that carry donor restrictions would not be considered current assets. All assets that are not current are considered noncurrent assets.

A current liability is a liability that is expected to be satisfied with current assets. All assets that are not current liabilities are noncurrent liabilities. As mentioned above, as noncurrent liabilities mature (or when portions of noncurrent liabilities become due), these liabilities (or their current portions) become current liabilities.

Exhibits 2.1 and 2.2 provide two examples of statements of financial position. Exhibit 2.1 illustrates liquidity by presenting a classified balance sheet, meaning that amounts are classified as current assets and liabilities. Exhibit 2.2 illustrates providing information about liquidity by the sequencing of assets and liabilities.

STATEMENT OF ACTIVITIES

The statement of activities presents the increases and decreases to a not-for-profit organization's net assets over a period of time. For fiscal year financial statements, the statement of activities presents the increases and decreases in net assets over the entire fiscal year. The concept of increases and decreases in net assets may be a technically pure definition of this statement's contents. A non-accountant might understand this statement better if it were termed the *operating* statement or the *income* statement.

Information on Changes in Net Assets

The statement of activities reports all increases and decreases in net assets during the year, meaning that the net assets at the beginning of the year, plus or minus the net change in net assets, should equal the net assets at the end of the fiscal period, as reported in the statement of financial position. Not only must the statement of activities provide the increases and decreases in net assets in total, it must also report the increases and decreases separately for each of the three classifications of net assets—unrestricted, temporarily restricted, and permanently restricted. Not-for-profit organizations that have temporarily restricted and permanently restricted net assets usually choose the multicolumn format for presenting their statements of activities. Increases and decreases in unrestricted, temporarily restricted, and permanently restricted net assets are each included in a separate column with

EXHIBIT 2.1 Classified statement of financial position

The Museum of Accounting
Statement of Financial Position
September 30, 20X1

Assets

Current assets:

Cash and cash equivalents	$xxx
Short-term investments	xxx
Contributions receivable	xxx
Unrestricted	xxx
Temporarily restricted	xxx
Total contributions receivable	xxx
Accounts receivable	xxx
Prepaid expenses	xxx
Total current assets	xxx
Deposits	xxx
Property and equipment	xxx
Total assets	$xxx

Liabilities

Current liabilities:

Current portion of long-term debt	$xxx
Accounts payable	xxx
Accrued expenses	xxx
Total current liabilities	xxx
Long-term debt less current portion	xxx
Total liabilities	xxx

Net Assets

Unrestricted	xxx
Temporarily restricted	xxx
Permanently restricted	xxx
Total net assets	xxx
Total liabilities and net assets	$xxx

EXHIBIT 2.2   Sequenced statement of financial position

The Museum of Accounting
Statement of Financial Position
September 30, 20X1

Assets

Cash and cash equivalents	$xxx
Accounts receivable	xxx
Unrestricted contributions receivable	xxx
Short-term investments	xxx
Prepaid expenses	xxx
Assets restricted to payment of long-term debt	xxx
Deposits on property	xxx
Property and equipment	xxx
Assets restricted for permanent endowment	xxx
Total assets	$xxx

Liabilities

Accounts payable	$xxx
Accrued expenses	xxx
Long-term debt	xxx
Total liabilities	xxx

Net Assets

Unrestricted	xxx
Temporarily restricted	xxx
Permanent restricted	xxx
Total net assets	xxx
Total liabilities and net assets	$xxx

the total of all three presented in an additional total column. For comparative purposes, the total column from the prior fiscal year's statement of activities is often presented to provide prior year information. Presenting each increase and decrease in each of the classifications of net assets for the prior fiscal year would usually make this statement unwieldy. (Exhibit 2.3 on page 54 presents a sample of a not-for-profit organization's statement of activities using the multicolumn format.)

The increases and decreases in net assets reported in the statement of activities result from these types of transactions:

- Revenues
- Expenses
- Gains and losses
- Reclassifications

The definitions and discussions of revenues, expenses, and gains and losses were provided in Chapter 1. The concept of *reclassification* is a financial reporting mechanism in which one classification of net assets increases and another classification of net assets decreases, with no change in the total net assets of the not-for-profit organization.

Reclassifications are reported on the statement of activities to reflect the satisfaction of donor restrictions. As described in Chapter 1, revenues of not-for-profit organizations can increase unrestricted, temporarily restricted, or permanently restricted net assets. Expenses of a not-for-profit organization are recorded as decreases in unrestricted net assets. As donor restrictions are satisfied (their time or purpose temporary restrictions are met), the related net assets are reclassified from temporarily restricted to unrestricted. This decreases temporarily restricted net assets (which makes sense, because there are fewer assets that are restricted by donors) and increases unrestricted net assets (which makes sense, because not only have the donor restrictions been satisfied, but the expenses related to these contributions are recorded as unrestricted net assets). Another way of looking at reclassifications of temporarily restricted net assets to unrestricted net assets is simply that the restrictions have been satisfied and the assets need to be reclassified in the financial statements.

Reporting Revenues and Expenses on a Gross Basis

Prior to the issuance of SFAS 117, not-for-profit organizations sometimes offset the expenses from some activities against the revenues generated by those activities and only reflected the net amounts in their financial statements. SFAS 117 requires that, for not-for-profit organizations' major and central operating activities, revenues and expenses be recorded on a gross basis, meaning that offsetting revenues and expenses is not allowed.

The types of activities where netting would be appropriate would include investment activities, where investment expenses may be offset against investment earnings, with only the net amount reported. In a similar way, investment gains and losses may be netted in the calculation of investment income for purposes of financial reporting. In addition, other minor transactions that are incidental to the operation of a not-for-profit organization may be netted. For the most part, reporting gross amounts is the preference of SFAS 117 and the financial statement reader would be correct in questioning financial statements which present more than these types of transactions on a net basis.

Exhibit 2.3 provides an example of a sample statement of activities in a multicolumn format for a not-for-profit organization.

Functional Reporting

One of the most important aspects of the statement of activities for not-for-profit organizations is the requirement for functional reporting, as required by SFAS 117. While not-for-profit organizations may present this information in the notes to the financial statements, this discussion assumes that the functional reporting

EXHIBIT 2.3   Sample statement of activities in a multicolumn format

The Helping Hand Children's Organization
Statement of Activities
Year Ended June 30, 20X1
(in thousands)

	Unrestricted	Temporarily restricted	Permanently restricted	Total
Revenues, gains, and other support:				
Contributions	$xxx	$xxx	$xxx	$xxx
Fees	xxx			xxx
Income on long-term investments	xxx	xxx	xxx	xxx
Other investment income	xxx			xxx
Net unrealized and realized gains on long-term investments	xxx	xxx	xxx	xxx
Other	xxx			xxx
Net assets released from restrictions				
Satisfaction of program restrictions	xxx	(xxx)		
Satisfaction of equipment acquisition restrictions	xxx	(xxx)		
Expiration of time restrictions	xxx	(xxx)		
Total revenues, gains, and other support	xxx	(xxx)	xxx	xxx
Expenses and losses:				
Program A	xxx			xxx
Program B	xxx			xxx
Program C	xxx			xxx
Management and general	xxx			xxx
Fund-raising	xxx			xxx
Total expenses	xxx			xxx
Fire loss	xxx			xxx
Actuarial loss on annuity obligations		xxx		xxx
Total expenses and losses	xxx	xxx		xxx
Change in net assets	xxx	(xxx)	xxx	xxx
Net assets at beginning of year	xxx	xxx	xxx	xxx
Net assets at end of year	$xxx	$xxx	$xxx	$xxx

information is included on the face of the statement of activities. Irrespective of where it is reported, the concepts described in the following paragraphs would apply.

Functional reporting, as its name implies, describes the activity for which the not-for-profit organization incurred the expense. The functional classifications that must be used are:

- Program expenses
- Supporting service expenses, which are further classified as:
  - Management and general expenses
  - Fund-raising expenses
  - Membership development expenses

Program Expenses

Program expenses relate to those program service activities that result in services (or goods) being distributed to beneficiaries, cus-tomers, or members that fulfill the basic mission of the not-for-profit organization. Program services are the reasons that not-for-profit organizations exist. They are the major output of the organization. An organization can (and frequently does) have more than one category of program services. For example, a children's services agency might have a day-care program, an after-school homework program, and a summer camp. A country club may have a golf program, tennis program, and a catering program. Each of these are program services and the not-for-profit organization is likely to report each of these separately. While GAAP may be clearer as to what are program services versus supporting services, more judgment is required in determining how many different types of program services to report. Any more than four or five types of program services may be too many and start to cloud the information presented, as well as pose too large of a bookkeeping effort.

Tip Not-for-profit organizations usually err on the side of recording an expense as a program expense instead of as a supporting service expense. The larger the percentage of total expenses that program service expenses comprise, the more efficient and effective the not-for-profit organization appears.

Management and General Expenses

Management and general expenses as contemplated by SFAS 117 relate to activities such as oversight, business management, general record keeping, and budgeting and financing (including related administrative activities). Basically, any expense that is not directly related to a program activity, fund-raising, or membership development is considered part of management and general expenses. Two expenses that should be considered part of management and general expenses are those expenses related to the activities of the organization's board of directors and those related to the organization's annual report. In addition, expenses incurred in obtaining revenues from exchange transactions should be considered management and general expenses and not fund-raising expenses. Exchange transaction revenues are those fee-for-service activities described in Chapter 1.

In some cases, costs are incurred for activities that are related to more than one functional category. There are specific rules as to when and how these costs can be allocated. This topic is covered in Chapter 5. Certain other costs, for example, result in direct expenses in more than one functional category. For example, a not-for-profit organization may report the salary and fringe benefit expenses of its executive director as management and general expenses. Another not-for-profit organization, on the other hand, may be able to discern between the executive director's time spent on program activities, management and general activities, and fund-raising activities. With the assistance of some form of timekeeping mechanism, the not-for-profit organization is able to determine the amount of time the executive director spends on each of these activities and then directly allocate a portion of the executive director's salary and fringe benefit expenses to each of these activities. These examples are illustrative only and not meant to suggest that only the executive director's salary and fringe benefit expenses can be allocated in this way. It is intended to introduce the concept of direct cost allocation as a way of understanding how costs are accumulated into the functional classifications that are being described. There may be other employees whose time may be allocated to different functions. For example, in a larger not-for-profit organization, one or more members of the accounting department may spend all or an identifiable part of their time processing a specific type of transaction for a particular program. There is nothing that would preclude their salary costs from being fully or partially charged directly as a program expense as long as their time allocation could be documented and the method of allocation consistently applied.

Fund-raising Expenses

Fund-raising expenses are those expenses incurred in inducing donors to contribute to the not-for-profit organization. The types of activities that are included in the fund-raising category will vary among different not-for-profit organizations. Some of the more common fund-raising activities highlighted by SFAS 117 include publicizing and conducting fund-raising campaigns; maintaining donor mailing lists; conducting special fund-raising events; preparing and distributing fund-raising manuals, instructions, and other materials. Fund-raising activities include those involving soliciting contributions not just from individuals but also from businesses, foundations, and governments.

Tip   Not-for-profit organizations generally prefer not to report a high level of fund-raising expenses. Not-for-profit organizations that report little or no fund-raising expenses but report significant contributions and support revenues may be reporting the expenses of some fund-raising activities in management and general, or worse, in program services.

Membership Development Expenses

Membership development activities and their related expenses are only found in not-for-profit organizations that are membership organizations. These activities include soliciting for prospective members and membership dues, membership relations, and similar types of activities.

Functional Reporting and Natural Expense Reporting

The distinction between functional reporting (described earlier) and natural expense reporting (that is, the reporting of expenses such as salaries, rent, utilities, etc.) is described in Chapter 1. SFAS 117 has an additional reporting requirement for voluntary health and welfare organizations, which is to provide an additional financial statement (or supplemental schedule to the financial statements) that is a matrix showing expenses in both their natural and functional classifications. This matrix is easier to see than describe, so a sample is provided as Exhibit 2.4.

This statement is required to be presented by voluntary health and welfare organizations, while all other not-for-profit organizations are encouraged to include this information within their basic financial statements. SFAS 117 defines what it considers to be voluntary health and welfare organizations that would be bound by this requirement. These are organizations that are formed for the purpose of performing voluntary services for various segments of society. They are tax-exempt (meaning that they are formed for the benefit of the public) and are operated on a not-for-profit basis. Most of these organizations concentrate their efforts and spend their resources in an attempt to solve health and welfare problems of society and individuals. Voluntary health and welfare organizations include those not-for-profit organizations that derive their revenue primarily from voluntary contributions from the general public to be used for general or specific purposes connected with health, welfare, or community services.

EXHIBIT 2.4 Statement of functional expenses

The Helping Hand Children's Organization
Statement of Functional Expenses
Year Ended June 30, 20X1

	Program A	Program B	Program C	Total program expenses	Management & general	Fund-raising	Total expenses
Personnel expenses:							
Executive salaries	$xxx	$xxx	$xxx	$xxx	$xxx	$xxx	$xxx
Support salaries	—	xxx	—	xxx	xxx	—	xxx
Hourly staff	—	xxx	—	xxx	—	—	xxx
Payroll taxes and benefits	xxx	xxx	xxx	xxx	xxx	xxx	xxx
Total personnel expenses	xxx	xxx	xxx	xxx	xxx	xxx	xxx
Direct expenses:							
Rent and utilities	—	—	—	—	xxx	—	xxx
Interest	—	—	—	—	xxx	—	xxx
Depreciation	—	—	—	—	xxx	—	xxx
Insurance	—	xxx	xxx	xxx	xxx	—	xxx
Maintenance	—	—	—	—	xxx	—	xxx
Supplies	xxx	xxx	xxx	xxx	xxx	—	xxx
Professional fees	—	—	—	—	xxx	—	xxx
Office expenses	—	—	—	—	xxx	—	xxx
Telephone	—	—	—	—	xxx	—	xxx
Total direct expenses	xxx	xxx	xxx	xxx	xxx	—	xxx
Total expenses	$xxx	$xxx	$xxx	$xxx	$xxx	$xxx	$xxx

STATEMENT OF CASH FLOWS

The final financial statement included in a not-for-profit organization's complete set of financial statements prepared in accordance with GAAP is the statement of cash flows. Prior to SFAS 117, many not-for-profit organizations did not prepare cash flow statements. SFAS 117 basically made the requirements of Statement of Financial Accounting Standards No. 95, "Statement of Cash Flows" (SFAS 95) applicable to not-for-profit organizations, with a slight bit of fine-tuning.

The cash flow statement provides information about the not-for-profit organization's receipts and disbursements of cash. While this principle sounds fairly easy to apply, there are some specific guidelines as to how this information is presented. Cash receipts and disbursements in the cash flow statement are classified into three categories of activities:

- Operating activities
- Investing activities
- Financing activities

This information is meant to assist creditors, donors, and others in assessing the ability of the organization to meet its cash needs, and presents the cash activities of the organization to provide additional information about how the organization receives and spends its cash. The statement of cash flows, similar to the statement of activities, is prepared for a period of time, generally the entire fiscal year of the not-for-profit organization. The cash at the beginning of the year, plus or minus all of the cash receipts and disbursements reported in the statement of cash flows, should equal the ending cash balance, as reported on the statement of financial position.

Definition of Cash

While the term *cash* in relation to the cash flow statement may appear obvious, it is not as obvious as it seems. For purposes of the statement of cash flows, cash includes not only the cash held by the not-for-profit organization in its bank account(s), but also its cash equivalents. Cash equivalents are short-term, highly liquid investments that are both (1) readily convertible to known amounts of cash and (2) so near their maturity that they present an insignificant risk of changes in value because of changes in interest rates. While the application of the exact definition of cash equivalents is beyond the scope of this discussion, suffice it to say that for an investment to be considered a cash equivalent, it must be virtually free of the risk that changes in interest rates will affect the fair value of the investment.

Categories of Cash Receipts and Disbursements

Earlier, the three categories of activities of cash receipts and disbursements were listed. The following sections will provide a general definition of what goes in each category and examples of cash receipts and disbursements typically found in each category.

Operating Activities

The operating activities reported in the statement of financial position reflect all cash transactions that are not classified as either investing or financing activities. This category would include cash receipts from general contributions received from donors as well as cash received from providing goods or services in fee-for-service revenue transactions.

Cash inflows from operating activities include:

- Contributions (other than long-term restricted contributions)
- Grants
- Receipts from the sales of goods or services

Cash outflows from operating activities include:

- Disbursements made for program activities
- Disbursements to employees, vendors, and contractors
- Payments of interest and taxes
- Grants made by the organization to other organizations

Cash flows from operating activities can be calculated using one of two methods: the direct method or the indirect method. While the mechanics of the calculation are beyond the scope of this book, readers should have a general idea of the differences between the two methods, which result in different financial statement presentations. The direct method reports actual receipts and disbursements for each item of cash inflow and outflow. The net cash provided by or used in operating activities is reconciled to the operating activities reported in the statement of activities. The indirect method begins with the result of operating activities reported in the statement of activities and then adjusts this amount to convert it to a cash receipts/disbursements basis. For example, depreciation is recorded as an expense in the statement of activities, but it does not result in a cash outflow. On the other hand, the purchase of a fixed asset results in a cash outflow, but does not result in an expense at acquisition, since the fixed asset is recorded as an asset on the statement of financial position. While the direct method is the recommended one (by SFAS 95), most organizations use the indirect method, since it is easier to calculate.

Investing Activities

Investing activities include acquiring and disposing of debt and equity investments, making and collecting loans, and acquiring and disposing of property, plant, and equipment.

Cash inflows from investing activities include:

- Sales of property, plant, and equipment
- Collections on loans

Cash outflows for investing activities include:

- Purchases of property, plant, and equipment
- Disbursements of loans

Financing Activities

Financing activities include obtaining resources from owners and providing them with a return on (and/or a return of) their investment. Financing activities also include borrowing money and repaying amounts borrowed, as well as obtaining and paying for other resources obtained from creditors using long-term credit. While not-for-profit organizations do not have owners to whom they pay a rate of return (they might have some serious tax problems if they did), they *do* borrow money and use long-term credit to buy resources. This category would also include cash received for contributions from donors that is restricted for long-term purposes for which the restrictions have not yet been satisfied and the cash is still being held.

Cash inflows from financing activities include:

- Receipts of contributions from donors that are restricted for long-term purposes
- Receipts from issuance of membership shares in a social or country club
- Interest and dividends restricted for long-term use
- Short- and long-term borrowings

Cash outflows from financing activities include:

- Repayments of short- and long-term debt
- Repayments of capital leases

Noncash Activities

While the title of the statement is the *cash flow statement*, the statement is required to report noncash transactions as well. The cash flow statement should include noncash investing and financing activities either by narrative or by the inclusion of a schedule of noncash transactions as part of the statement of cash flows. Not-for-profit organizations often receive gifts of marketable securities from donors, and these contributions would be noncash transactions that should be included as such in the statement of cash flows. Other examples of the types of transactions that might be found in the cash flow statement of a not-for-profit organization include acquiring a building by the assumption of a mortgage; obtaining an asset by entering into a capital lease; and contributions of land, buildings, equipment, or collection items by donors.

Exhibits 2.5 and 2.6 provide two examples of a statement of cash flows. Exhibit 2.5 is prepared using the direct method. Exhibit 2.6 is prepared using the indirect method.

Notes to the Financial Statements

Many readers of the financial statements of not-for-profit organizations overlook the importance of the notes that are part of those statements. The notes are not simply an add-on to basic financial statements—they are an integral part of the financial statements for a complete presentation in accordance with GAAP. The sources for the requirements of the notes to the financial statements are many. Each new FASB statement or pronouncement that is issued more often than not includes some new disclosure requirements that must be contained in the notes to the financial statements to address some specific aspect of the new statement or pronouncement.

In addition to the new notes required by new statements or pronouncements, there are some core notes that have must be included. One of the most significant notes, which should generally be the first note reported, is the summary of significant accounting policies. In certain instances, not-for-profit organizations can choose from among a number of acceptable accounting principles to use. Where such choice exists, the summary of significant

EXHIBIT 2.5 Illustration of a cash flow statement using the direct method

Institute of Accounting Theory
Statement of Cash Flows
For the Fiscal Year Ended June 30, 20X1

Cash flows from operating activities:	
Cash received from service recipients	$ xxx
Cash received from donors	xxx
Cash collected on contributions receivable	xxx
Interest and dividends received	xxx
Interest paid	(xxx)
Cash paid to employees and suppliers	(xxx)
Grants paid	(xxx)
Net cash provided by operating activities	xxx
Cash flows from investing activities:	
Purchases of equipment	(xxx)
Proceeds from sales of investments	xxx
Purchases of investments	(xxx)
Net cash used by investing activities	(xxx)
Cash flows from financing activities:	
Proceeds from contributions restricted for:	
Investment in endowment	xxx
Investment in plant	xxx
Investment subject to annuity agreements	xxx
	xxx
Other financing activities:	
Interest and dividends restricted for reinvestment	xxx
Payments on notes payable	(xxx)
Payments on long-term debt	(xxx)
	(xxx)
Net cash used by financing activities	(xxx)
Net increase in cash and cash equivalents	xxx
Cash and cash equivalents at beginning of year	xxx
Cash and cash equivalents at end of year	$ xxx
Reconciliation of change in net assets to net cash provided by operating activities:	
Change in net assets	$ xxx
Adjustments to reconcile change in net assets to net cash used by operating activities:	
Depreciation	xxx
Actuarial loss on annuity obligations	xxx
Increase in accounts and interest receivable	(xxx)
Decrease in contributions receivable	xxx
Increase in accounts payable	xxx
Decrease in grants payable	(xxx)
Contributions restricted for long-term investment	(xxx)
Interest and dividends restricted for long-term investment	(xxx)
Net unrealized and realized gains on long-term investment	(xxx)
Net cash provided by operating activities	$ xxx
Supplemental data for noncash investing and financing activities:	
Gifts of equipment	xxx

EXHIBIT 2.6 Illustration of a cash flow statement using the indirect method

Institute of Accounting Theory
Statement of Cash Flows
For the Fiscal Year Ended June 30, 20X1

Cash flows from operating activities:	
Change in net assets	$ xxx
Adjustments to reconcile change in net assets to net cash	
used by operating activities:	
Depreciation	xxx
Actuarial loss on annuity obligations	xxx
Increase in accounts and interest receivable	(xxx)
Decrease in contributions receivable	xxx
Increase in accounts payable	xxx
Decrease in grants payable	(xxx)
Contributions restricted for long-term investment	(xxx)
Interest and dividends restricted for long-term investment	(xxx)
Net unrealized and realized gains on long-term investments	(xxx)
Net cash provided by operating activities	xxx
Cash flows from investing activities:	
Purchase of equipment	(xxx)
Proceeds from sales of investments	xxx
Purchases of investments	(xxx)
Net cash used by investing activities	(xxx)
Cash flows from financing activities:	
Proceeds from contributions restricted for:	
Investment in endowment	xxx
Investment in plant	xxx
Investment subject to annuity agreements	xxx
Other financing activities:	
Interest and dividends restricted for reinvestment	xxx
Payments of annuity obligation	(xxx)
Payments on notes payable	(xxx)
Payments on long-term debt	(xxx)
Net cash used by financing activities	(xxx)
Net increase in cash and cash equivalents	xxx
Cash and cash equivalents at beginning of year	xxx
Cash and cash equivalents at end of year	$ xxx
Supplemental data:	
Noncash investing and financing activities:	
Gifts of equipment	xxx
Interest paid	xxx

accounting policies helps the reader understand what policies were chosen by the organization, which assists the reader in understanding the statements as well as in comparing them to those of another not-for-profit organization that may have used different acceptable principles. As will be described in Chapter 8, for example, a not-for-profit organization has a choice of several different approaches to account for collections of art or other historical treasures. The method selected should be disclosed and described in the notes to the financial statements. In some cases, there is a choice in selecting a method to comply with GAAP. For example, a not-for-profit organization must record depreciation on its fixed assets. There is no choice in that. However, there are a number of acceptable depreciation methods (straight-line, declining balance, sum-of-the-years digits, etc.) that are acceptable methods for calculating depreciation under GAAP. In other cases, the application of accounting principles requires certain assumptions and decisions to be made by the financial statement preparer. The summary of significant accounting policies, as well as some of the other notes, are important mechanisms to disclose these application options to the reader of the financial statements.

A detailed discussion of the various disclosure requirements under GAAP is far beyond the scope of this book, although many of the required disclosures will be covered as specific accounting topics are addressed in the remainder of the book. The important point to be made to the non-accountant in trying to read and understand not-for-profit organization financial statements, however, is the very important nature of the notes to the financial statements, which provide a key to understanding the amounts and activities reported in the statements of financial position, activities, and cash flows.

SUMMARY

This chapter provided a basic discussion of the financial statements of a not-for-profit organization prepared in accordance with GAAP. This understanding, coupled with the accounting basics in Chapter 1, provide the reader with a basic framework for not-for-profit accounting and financial reporting. The balance of this book is devoted to examining specific accounting topics, some of which are only applicable to not-for-profit organizations, and some of which are applicable to not-for-profit and commercial enterprises. The framework provided in Chapter 1 and this chapter, coupled with the specific accounting topic information provided in the balance of this book, will provide the non-accountant with a very usable understanding of not-for-profit accounting and financial reporting.

CHAPTER 3

Accounting for Contributions

Contributions from donors are the lifeblood of most not-for-profit organizations. In many cases, they are an organization's only significant source of income. Accounting for contributions is complicated because donors often attach "strings" to their contributions, and these strings sometimes have an impact on the way in which a contribution is accounted for by a not-for-profit organization. (Later in this chapter, *strings* will be categorized as donor conditions and donor restrictions.)

This chapter discusses these topics, which are key to understanding the correct accounting and financial reporting for contributions:

- When contributions should be recorded
- Understanding the impact of donor restrictions on the reporting of contributions
- Accounting for contributed services
- Accounting for other noncash contributions
- Pass-through contributions

An understanding of these basic concepts will enable the non-accountant to understand and analyze how not-for-profit organizations report contributions in their financial statements, including the impact of donor-imposed conditions and restrictions. Many of the accounting concepts discussed in this chapter are based on

FASB Statement No. 116, "Accounting for Contributions Received and Contributions Made" (SFAS 116), which, as its name implies, is an entire FASB statement devoted solely to the accounting for contributions by not-for-profit organizations.

WHEN SHOULD CONTRIBUTIONS BE RECORDED?

Determining when a contribution should be recorded sounds like an easy task. The not-for-profit organization should record the contribution in the fiscal year that it receives the contribution. If it was as simple as that, this would be a pretty short chapter. To start the discussion, let's first look at the definition of *contribution* as contemplated by SFAS 116.

Contribution Definition

Continuing with the examination of the actual meanings of complicated accounting definitions started in Chapter 1, let us start with SFAS 116's definition of a contribution: "A contribution is an unconditional transfer of cash or other assets to an entity or a settlement or cancellation of its liabilities in a voluntary nonreciprocal transfer by another entity acting other than as an owner. Other assets include securities, land, buildings, use of facilities or utilities, materials and supplies, intangible assets, services, and unconditional promises to give those items in the future." The two most important terms in this definition for determining when a contribution is recorded are "unconditional transfer" and the inclusion of "unconditional promises to give" as one of the other assets included in the definition of a contribution.

Unconditional Transfers

In order for a contribution to be recorded as revenue by a not-for-profit organization, the transfer (whether cash or another asset) must be unconditional. That means it can have no donor-imposed conditions on whether or not the not-for-profit organization gets to keep the asset. According to SFAS 116, a donor-imposed condition is: "A donor stipulation that specifies a future and uncertain event whose occurrence or failure to occur gives the promisor a right of return of the assets it has transferred or releases the promisor from its obligation to transfer its assets." This means that if the not-for-profit organization's right to keep the contribution is dependent on some future event that may or may not occur, the not-for-profit should not record this contribution as revenue.

Practical Example   A donor contributes $100,000 to a fund-raising campaign for the not-for-profit to build a new building at a cost of $1 million. The donor stipulates that unless the not-for-profit raises the additional $900,000 from the fund-raising campaign and is able to build the building, the donor will receive its $100,000 back from the not-for-profit organization. There is an uncertain event in the future (raising $900,000 and being able to build the building). The not-for-profit organization would record the cash received ($100,000) as an asset with a corresponding amount as a liability (deferred revenue). When the donor's conditions are met (i.e., the additional $900,000 is raised and the building is built), the not-for-profit organization will eliminate the $100,000 of deferred revenue recorded on its statement of financial position and record $100,000 as contribution revenue.

Note that, in the above example, the donor has imposed *conditions*, not *restrictions*. In this example, if the donor had simply stipulated that the $100,000 be used for the building, it would have restricted the use of the asset, but it would *not* have attached conditions to the contributions. (Restricted contributions will be discussed later in this chapter.)

Summarizing the accounting implications of donor-imposed conditions, the not-for-profit organization would record the asset received, but would record a liability (deferred revenue) on its statement of financial position until such time as the donor's conditions were met. Once they were met, the deferred revenue amount would be removed from the statement of financial position and contribution revenue would be recognized in the organization's statement of activities. If the contribution received was unconditional, the asset received would be recorded when received and contribution revenue would be recorded as an increase in net assets on the statement of activities when the contribution was received.

Promises to Give

Referring to the definition of contributions provided earlier in this chapter, it was noted that the second important term was "unconditional promises to give" as one of the other assets that would be considered a contribution. This has a very significant impact on when contributions are recorded as revenue by not-for-profit organizations. The promise itself becomes the contribution. The actual cash or other asset that will ultimately be given to the not-for-profit organization will be provided by the donor at a later time. Note that the term included in the other asset definition is "unconditional." If the promise to give is not unconditional, it would not be recognized in the not-for-profit organization's financial statements.

This provision of SFAS 116 had a very significant impact on the timing of the recognition of contribution revenue. Prior to SFAS 116, it would be safe to say that many not-for-profit organizations were reluctant to record donor promises as contribution revenue. These organizations preferred to wait to record the contribution until the donor actually provided the gift that it intended to make. SFAS 116 requires that unconditional promises to give be recorded as contribution revenue (assuming that they are expected to be collected, which is discussed later in this section).

In order for a promise to give to be unconditional and require recording, SFAS 116 provides a specific definition of an unconditional promise to give as: "A promise to give is a written or oral agreement to contribute cash or other assets to another entity; however, to be recognized in the financial statements there must be sufficient evidence in the form of verifiable documentation that a promise was made and received. A communication that does not indicate clearly whether it is a promise is considered an unconditional promise to give if it indicates an unconditional intention to give that is legally enforceable."

Tip   Whether an unconditional promise to give is sufficiently documented and verifiable is a matter of judgment for financial statement preparers and their independent auditors. However, fund-raising management should ensure that, where it is the not-for-profit organization's intention to record an unconditional promise to give as a contribution, sufficient evidence is received from the donor. Development of standardized forms and letters is recommended, along with input from accountants and independent auditors, if deemed necessary. This will serve to avoid any confusion among the financial statement preparer, the independent auditor, and perhaps more importantly, the donor, about whether or not a promise to give is unconditional.

The actual documentation and its verifiability will generally vary with the size and the nature of the promise to give (often called a *pledge* by not-for-profit organizations). Certainly, a $5-million promise to give $1 million each year for five years will be documented differently than a $25 pledge received from cold-calling potential donors as part of a telephone fund-raising campaign. That is why the professional judgment used in recording pledges becomes key in making sure that only pledges as contemplated by SFAS 116 are recorded.

Valuation of Unconditional Promises to Give

A promise to make a contribution in the future is worth less than an immediate cash contribution for financial reporting purposes because of the time value of money. That is why SFAS 116 specifies that unconditional promises to give cash should be recorded in the financial statements at the time of the promise at their present value of the estimated future cash flows. Simply stated, a $1 contribution expected to be received in one year might be recorded at, say, $.92 now. The reason is that the not-for-profit would be able to invest that $.92 now and, assuming an interest rate that is similar to a rate that the not-for-profit organization could have received from investing its asset (known as the discount rate), would be able to turn the $.92 into $1 over the one-year time period. Although specific present value calculations are beyond the scope of this book, where the unconditional promise involves a payment stream (for example, the $1 million received each year for five years in a previous example), the present value concept can be applied to reflect that different amounts of the promise to give will be uncollected for different time periods. Note that these calculations are based on the *estimated* future cash flows, which may or may not be the actual amounts unconditionally promised by the donor. See the discussion below of net realizable value for factors to consider in determining what cash flows are ultimately expected to be received from the donor and why they may differ from the amounts promised.

SFAS 116 does provide some relief to these present value calculations in that if the cash is expected to be received from the donor in less than one year, the present value calculations are not required because they won't produce a contribution amount too significantly different from what will ultimately be received.

One important point that should not be overlooked, however, is that, in cases where the present value calculations are not necessary, it is *not* automatically the promised amount to give that is recorded. The amount recorded should be the *net realizable value.* How does net realizable value differ from the amount that the donor promised to give? In many cases it will not because the not-for-profit organization will expect to receive what the donor promises to give. In other cases, however, donors do not always give what they promise to give. Sometimes a not-for-profit can use past experience to predict that a particular donor historically only pays 50% or 75% of what was originally promised. The not-for-profit would record the amount expected to be received as a contribution, not the amount of the actual promise.

Although a not-for-profit organization may be able to legally enforce the promise against a donor, it does not always make business sense to do so, since it is likely to scare off many donors from ever making a pledge to the organization. Imagine making a $25 pledge that is part of a telephone fund-raising campaign for a not-for-profit organization, and then subsequently changing your mind about the contribution and not paying the pledge. Even if the not-for-profit organization has a legal right to enforce the claim, it's probably not worth their while. Turning your unpaid pledge over to a collection agency would be another highly effective method of alienating a future potential donor forever. Chances are that the not-for-profit organization will send several reminders, and, if not paid, just forget about the pledge.

In addition, sometimes the financial condition of the donor changes from the time that the unconditional promise to give is made and when the cash is expected to be received by the not-for-profit organization. Taking legal action to collect an unconditional promise to give against a bankrupt donor may not result in collections that justify an expensive legal proceeding. As this book is being written, the stock market is trading well off its all-time highs, business conditions have deteriorated, many of the so-called dot.com companies that produced almost instant millionaires (on paper) are now bankrupt, and the instant millionaires are no longer. While this is a fairly recent occurrence that may not be repeated for a while, there are always ups and downs in the business cycle and, during harder economic times, it can be expected that some donors will not be able to fulfill their pledges. Not-for-profit organizations are feeling and will continue to feel the effects of the economic conditions, and the net realizable values of many unconditional promises to give will be much smaller than the original amounts promised. The accounting for these promises should anticipate that these types of circumstances can occur.

While the above discussion focuses on larger contributions, not-for-profit organizations also raise significant amounts of money through numerous smaller donations. These small amounts are sometimes obtained through telethons and other organized efforts to obtain pledges for future cash contributions. The accounting question is whether a not-for-profit organization should record these types of small pledges as receivables and contribution revenue when the pledge is made. The answer is *yes*, assuming that these pledges are unconditional. However, the discussion on net realizable value above must be considered, because it is likely that not every donor is going to honor every pledge. The not-for-profit organization should record the pledges as receivables, but at the same time record an allowance for uncollectible pledges, which, at the end of the fiscal year, would equal the amount of the as-yet uncollected pledges that the not-for-profit organization never expects to collect. This estimate of how much of these pledges will never be received should be based on past history with similar fundraising efforts.

From a financial management perspective, a not-for-profit organization would want to be fairly conservative in estimating the net realizable value of its receivables. Conservative in this respect means estimating the net realizable value on the lower end of a range of values that would be acceptable under GAAP. While there may be some in the not-for-profit organization who would want to show as good a result from a fund-raising effort as possible, overstating the amount that will ultimately be collected from receivables causes the not-for-profit organization to spend or commit to spend resources that it may ultimately not have because it is unable to collect.

UNDERSTANDING THE IMPACT OF DONOR RESTRICTIONS ON THE REPORTING OF CONTRIBUTIONS

Chapter 1 defines the three different net asset classifications used by not-for-profit organizations—unrestricted, temporarily restricted, and permanently restricted. Both temporarily restricted and permanently restricted net assets arise because of donor restrictions. Since expenses of not-for-profit organizations are paid out of unrestricted assets, and fee-for-service activities are not performed for donors, contributions are the transactions that give rise to temporarily restricted and permanently restricted net assets. (Note that investment income on temporarily and permanently restricted net assets may also be restricted, but more about that later.)

Temporary Restrictions

To briefly review, a temporary restriction is a donor-imposed restriction that permits a not-for-profit organization to use or spend donated assets as specified. Temporary restrictions are satisfied either by the passage of time or by actions of the organization. Temporary restrictions are more specific than the broad limits that result from the nature of the organization. For example, making a gift to a not-for-profit homeless shelter that is not otherwise restricted would not make this contribution restricted simply because its use is limited to providing services to the homeless. The broad nature of the organization, its operating environment, and its purposes in its articles of incorporation or bylaws are specifically identified in SFAS 116 as not giving rise to donor restrictions. To be considered temporarily restricted, the donor would have to specify either when the asset could be spent or used by the organization or for what purpose the asset could be used.

Sometimes a time restriction imposed by a donor that makes a contribution during the year is satisfied by the not-for-profit organization before the end of the fiscal year. In these cases, the contribution can be recorded as unrestricted in the fiscal year financial statements, instead of recorded as restricted and then reclassified as unrestricted during the same financial reporting period. In addition, a pledge received from a donor that is not due until sometime in the future should be recorded as a temporarily restricted asset until such time as the contribution is due from the donor, at which time the contributed asset should be reclassified to unrestricted net assets.

Not-for-profit organizations that receive gifts of long-lived assets must set an accounting policy as to whether or not these contributions are considered temporarily restricted because of a time restriction. Some organizations adopt a policy that a contributed long-lived asset (let us say a car) that has a life of five years is temporarily restricted because it must be used over a five-year period. Other organizations adopt a policy that the same contribution would be recorded as unrestricted. Either approach is acceptable under SFAS 116, although the policy should be disclosed in the notes to the financial statements.

Permanent Restrictions

A permanent restriction on a contribution is one in which a donor stipulates that resources be maintained permanently, but permits the organization to use or spend part or all of the income derived from the donated assets. In some cases, donors make gifts to a not-for-profit organization and specify that the not-for-profit organization must hold the gift in perpetuity. In the more well-known example, usually called an endowment, a gift of cash or securities is made that the organization will invest (or keep invested). Income derived from the permanently restricted assets is then available for use by the not-for-profit organization. The income may be unrestricted or may be temporarily restricted. For example, if an endowment is given to an educational institution and the income from the investments is restricted to provide scholarships to students, the principal of the endowment is permanently restricted and, until the scholarships are actually made, the income from the endowment is temporarily restricted. In other cases, the income from endowment funds is not temporarily restricted and can be used by the not-for-profit organization in the same way as its other unrestricted assets.

ACCOUNTING FOR CONTRIBUTED SERVICES

Not-for-profit organizations often use the work of volunteers to assist the organization in fulfilling its mission. Some organizations obtain their legal services on a pro bono basis. Others may obtain certain consulting services for free. Should these not-for-profit organizations record the value of these services as a contribution (with a corresponding expense for the use of this contribution)? The answer is: *It depends.* SFAS 116 provides that if certain conditions are met, the value of contributed services should be recognized (that is, recorded as contribution revenue with a corresponding increase in a fixed asset or in an expense) in the financial statements. If the SFAS 116 conditions are not met for recognition in the financial statements, the not-for-profit organization may disclose the nature and value of these services in the notes to the financial statements.

Contributed services should be recognized in the financial statements if the services received meet one of these criteria:

- Create or enhance the value of a nonfinancial asset
- Require specialized skills, are provided by individuals possessing those skills, and would typically be purchased if not provided by donation

Creating or enhancing the value of a nonfinancial asset should be fairly easy to identify and value. If a local contractor agrees to renovate the offices of a not-for-profit organization for the cost of materials only, the value of the contributed labor should be considered a contribution and, in this case, added to the capitalized cost of the building. The services should be valued at their fair value, which may be obtained in consultation with the contractor or by obtaining estimates from other contractors as to what they would normally charge for these services.

As for the requirement for specialized skills, SFAS 116 provides some examples of what it considers to be services requiring specialized skills. These are services provided by accountants, architects, carpenters, doctors, electricians, lawyers, nurses, plumbers, teachers and other professionals, and craftsmen.

ACCOUNTING FOR OTHER NONCASH CONTRIBUTIONS

As can be learned from the above discussion, contributions to not-for-profit organizations are not always in the form of cash (or a promise to pay cash in the future). Sometimes the contributions are for services and sometimes the contributions are for noncash assets. Noncash assets received by not-for-profit organizations should be recorded as contributions in the same way that cash contributions are. They should be categorized as unrestricted, temporarily restricted, or permanently restricted.

The accounting question for recording noncash contributions often centers around what value to record as the amount of the contribution. The basic rule is that noncash contributions are reported at their fair value. Determining the actual fair value (this used to be referred to as fair market value) may be easy or difficult, depending on the nature of the asset.

One of the more common noncash contributions received by not-for-profit organizations is investment securities. There are tax and other advantages available to donors when they donate appreciated securities to not-for-profit organizations, resulting in the broad popularity of this noncash contribution. In most cases, a readily determinable quoted market price is available for these securities and fair value for accounting purposes can be easily determined. In the case of debt securities, a market price may not be available for a particular bond, but fair values of bonds with similar stated interest rates, maturities, and credit risk are probably readily available. Other types of investments, such as restricted stock, stock in closely held corporations, limited partnership interests, and so on, may present more challenges in determining their fair value and, in these cases, experts (such as appraisers) may be needed to determine a reasonable fair value.

Other noncash contributions to not-for-profit organizations

may include many different types of assets, from real estate to inventory. Determining the level of effort needed to determine fair value will depend on the type and significance of the asset. For example, a not-for-profit organization that is the recipient of a contribution of 15 acres of land to build a summer camp for needy children is likely to spend more time and money determining the fair value of the donation (by obtaining appraisals, comparable sale information, etc.) than would a hospital auxiliary's resale clothing shop that accepts a donation of two bags of used clothes. Also to keep in mind is that, while the above discussions and examples of noncash contributions focus on contributions of assets, forgiveness of liabilities by donors is also a noncash contribution. In most cases, these are easier to value since the liability that is being forgiven is recorded (hopefully) as a liability on the statement of financial condition of the not-for-profit organization, thus providing a value for the noncash contribution.

Another form of noncash contributions received by some types of not-for-profit organizations, principally museums, is that of collections that include such items as historical treasures. The accounting for these types of contributions has its own rules, which are discussed in detail in Chapter 7.

PASS-THROUGH CONTRIBUTIONS

After the issuance of SFAS 116, some not-for-profit organizations that raise funds for other not-for-profit organizations questioned whether certain provisions of SFAS 116 would prevent these organizations from recording contribution revenue (and a corresponding expense) because they passed the funds that they raised through to the other organizations. Indeed, SFAS 116 states that it does not apply to ". . . transfers of assets in which the reporting entity acts as an agent, trustee, or intermediary, rather than as a donor or a donee." In other words, under this language, if a not-for-profit organization is an agent or an intermediary, it is not a donor or a donee, meaning that it does not have contribution revenue to record. The issue involved some of the not-for-profit organizations that are referred to as *federated fund-raising organizations.* These organizations obtain contributions from many individuals and other donors and then pass these funds through to many other not-for-profit organizations.

The accounting question is whether these not-for-profit organizations that pass through these contributions to other organizations should record the contributions as revenue, with a corresponding expense, when the funds were committed to the ultimate beneficiary organizations, or as a liability, which would then be decreased when the funds were sent to the ultimate beneficiary organizations. For these pass-through organizations, this is an important question because, without recording a revenue and expense, it would appear that they have virtually no program operations. Rather, their expenses would be all general and administrative and fund-raising. Fund-raising would appear even more abnormal, since they would have fund-raising expenses, but no contribution revenue. While the importance of this issue to not-for-profit organizations engaged solely in passing through contributions is clear, the issue also impacts other not-for-profit organizations that may have some pass-through activities in addition to their other program activities.

The accounting for pass-through activities was ultimately clarified by the issuance of FASB Statement No. 136, "Transfers of Assets to a Not-for-Profit Organization or Charitable Trust That Raises or Holds Contributions for Others" (SFAS 136). SFAS 136 applies to transactions where an entity (referred to as the donor) makes a contribution by transferring assets to a not-for-profit organization (referred to as the recipient organization) that accepts the assets from the donor and agrees to use the assets on behalf of, or transfer the assets to, the beneficiary that is specified by the donor. For example, Mr. Rich makes a contribution of $1,000 to his university alumni association, but specifies that the $1,000 be given by the alumni association to the university for use in its athletic scholarship fund. The accounting question centers on whether the alumni association would record the $1,000 as contribution revenue (and a $1,000 contribution expense) or whether it is merely acting as an agent or intermediary and should record a liability (instead of contribution revenue) because it owes the $1,000 to the university.

With two exceptions, which are described below, a recipient organization that accepts assets from a donor and agrees to use those assets on behalf of, or transfer those assets to, a specified beneficiary is not a donee. In these situations, the recipient organization should record an asset and a liability for cash and financial assets that it receives, measured at the fair value of the assets. When nonfinancial assets are received in this type of transaction, recording an asset and liability by the recipient is permitted, but not required. Whatever policy is adopted for nonfinancial assets should be disclosed and consistently applied.

The two exceptions to the above rules are described below. In these instances, the recipient organization would account for the transfer of assets as a donee (i.e., would record the receipt of assets as contribution revenue, instead of as a liability). Subsequent transfers to the assets to the ultimate beneficiary would then be accounted for as expenses (decreases in net assets) instead of a reduction to a liability.

1. A recipient organization acts as a donee (as opposed to an intermediary, trustee, or agent) if the donor explicitly grants the recipient organization variance power. Variance power is the unilateral power to redirect the use of the transferred assets to another beneficiary. SFAS 136 is clear that the variance power must be explicitly granted, meaning that the unilateral power to redirect the use of the assets is explicitly referred to in the instrument that transfers the assets. In addition, the variance power must be unilateral, meaning that the recipient organization can override the donor's instructions without the approval of the donor, specified beneficiary, or any other interested party.

2. If a recipient organization and a specified beneficiary are financially interrelated and the recipient organization is not a trustee, the recipient organization should record a con-

tribution when it receives assets from a donor that are specified for a beneficiary. SFAS 136 provides the example of a foundation that exists to raise, hold, and invest assets for a specified beneficiary, which generally is financially interrelated with the organization that it supports. In this example, the foundation recognizes contribution revenue when it receives assets from the donor. SFAS 136 prescribes that a recipient organization and the specified beneficiary are financially interrelated if their relationship has both of these characteristics:

- One organization has the ability to influence the operating and financial decisions of the other. Ways in which this influence may be demonstrated are:
  - The organizations are affiliates. (See Chapter 6 for a discussion of affiliate organizations.)
  - One organization has considerable representation on the governing board of the other organization.
  - The charter or bylaws of one organization limit its activities to those that are beneficial to the other organization.
  - An agreement between the organizations allows one organization to actively participate in the policy-making processes of the other, such as setting organizational priorities, budgets, and management compensation.
- One organization has an ongoing economic interest in the net assets of the other. If the specified beneficiary has an ongoing economic interest in the net assets of the recipient organization, the beneficiary's rights are residual. This means that the value of those rights increases or decreases as a result of the investment, fundraising, operating, or other activities of the recipient organization. A recipient organization may also have an ongoing economic interest in the net assets of the specified beneficiary. In that case, the recipient organization's rights would also be residual, meaning that their value changes as a result of the operations of the beneficiary.

SFAS 136 also provides guidance as to when specified beneficiaries would recognize their rights to assets held by recipient organizations. Specified beneficiaries should recognize their rights to assets (whether financial or nonfinancial) held by a recipient organization as an asset unless the recipient organization is explicitly granted variance power.

If the beneficiary and the recipient organization are financially interrelated organizations, the beneficiary should recognize its interest in the net assets of the recipient organization and adjust that interest for its share of the change in net assets of the recipient organization, similar to the equity method of accounting. If the beneficiary has an unconditional right to receive all or a portion of the specified cash flow from a charitable trust or other identifiable pool of assets, the beneficiary should recognize its beneficiary interest, measuring and subsequently remea-suring its interest at fair value. A valuation technique, such as the present value of the estimated expected future cash flows, should be used. In all other cases, a beneficiary recognizes its rights to the assets held by a recipient organization as a receivable and contribution revenue in accordance with the provisions of SFAS 116 for an unconditional promise to give. If a donor explicitly grants a recipient organization variance power, the specified un-affiliated beneficiary should not recognize its potential for future distributions from the assets held by the recipient organization.

In addition to the above guidance, SFAS 136 also specifies that a transfer of assets to a recipient organization is not a contribution and should be accounted for as an asset by the resource provider and as a liability by the recipient organization if one or more of these conditions exist:

- The transfer is subject to the resource provider's unilateral right to redirect the use of the assets to another beneficiary.
- The transfer is accompanied by the resource provider's conditional promise to give or is otherwise revocable or repayable.

- The resource provider controls the recipient organization and specifies an unaffiliated beneficiary.
- The resource provider specifies itself or its affiliates as the beneficiary, and the transfer is not an equity transaction.

For the purpose of the last condition above, a transfer of assets to a recipient organization is an equity transaction if all of these conditions specified by SFAS 136 are met:

- The resource provider specifies itself or its affiliate as the beneficiary.
- The resource provider and the recipient organization are financially interrelated organizations.
- Neither the resource provider nor its affiliate expects payment of the transferred assets, although payment of investment return on the transferred assets may be expected.

If a resource provider specifies itself as a beneficiary, it reports an equity transaction as an interest in the net assets of the recipient organization, or as an increase to a previously recognized interest. If the resource provider specifies an affiliate as a beneficiary, the resource provider reports an equity transaction as a separate line in its statement of activities, and the affiliate named as beneficiary reports an interest in the net assets of the recipient organization. A recipient organization should report an equity transaction as a separate line in its statement of activities.

This discussion of SFAS 136's rules is very detailed because SFAS 136 only allows pass-through organizations to recognize contribution revenues and expenses for contributions raised for others in two very limited circumstances—either the recipient organization has variance power or the recipient organization and the ultimate beneficiary are financially interrelated in such a way as is specified in SFAS 136. Keeping these two simple concepts in mind will help readers avoid getting entangled in the detailed requirements to such an extent that they lose sight of the basic concepts.

SUMMARY

Accounting for contributions is an area where there are a number of specific rules in GAAP that apply only to not-for-profit organizations. Understanding these requirements will enable the reader to understand the accounting for a significant number of transactions that not-for-profit organizations routinely record in their financial statements.

CHAPTER 4

Accounting for Investments and Financial Instruments

This chapter will focus on two important areas in generally accepted accounting principles for not-for-profit organizations: investments and financial instruments. The majority of not-for-profit organizations have investments of some type and the accounting and financial reporting for these investments is key to understanding not-for-profit organization accounting and financial reporting. (For the purpose of making this discussion as clear as possible, investments and financial instruments are treated separately, although a purist would point out that most investments are, in fact, a form of financial instruments.) Far fewer not-for-profit organizations have investments that are considered financial instruments (and indeed, not all types of financial instruments are investments or even assets), but there are relatively new accounting requirements for financial instruments, including derivatives, and the non-accountant needs—at a minimum—an overview of the accounting basics for these usually complex transactions.

Accordingly, the topics covered in this chapter are:

- Accounting for investments
- Accounting and financial reporting for financial instruments

As will be seen, accounting for investments has straightforward requirements that affect most not-for-profit organizations. Accounting for financial instruments has more complex requirements, but affects far fewer not-for-profit organizations.

ACCOUNTING FOR INVESTMENTS

Investments are commonly a significant part of the assets of many not-for-profit organizations. The reason is that donors often make gifts in the form of endowments (part of permanently restricted net assets, as was described in Chapter 3), in which the not-for-profit organization invests funds in perpetuity, while the income from the investments is used either on an unrestricted or temporarily restricted basis by the not-for-profit organization. Most of the endowment funds maintained by not-for-profit organizations are maintained in the form of investments. In addition to donor restrictions, sometimes the board of directors of a not-for-profit organization will designate certain funds (in the form of investments) to be set aside in what is commonly called a *board-designated investment fund.* In this case, a donor has not restricted the use of the assets and the assets are considered unrestricted. However, the board of directors may feel it is important for the not-for-profit organization to have a financial cushion and sets aside funds in a board-designated investment fund, which limits the management of the organization as to what, if any, funds can be removed from the board-designated fund. These types of funds can also be used by the board to assist the not-for-profit organization in accumulating funds for use in major projects, such as future long-term construction projects. Board-designated investment funds also result in not-for-profit organizations reporting significant amounts of investments on their statement of financial position.

Some investments of not-for-profit organizations are so liquid and have such short maturities that they are not classified on the statement of financial position as investments, but rather as cash equivalents. Cash equivalents would include money market funds, savings accounts, and some certificates of deposit and U.S. Treasury bills. Cash equivalents are discussed in Chapter 2 as part of the information presented on the statement of cash flows.

The area of investments is one in which there is a distinct FASB statement which governs the accounting and financial reporting for most, but not all, investments of not-for-profit organizations. This FASB statement is No. 124, "Accounting for Certain Investments Held by Not-for-Profit Organizations" (SFAS 124). Prior to SFAS 124, different types of not-for-profit organizations accounted for investments differently, depending on which American Institute of Certified Public Accountants (AICPA) Audit and Accounting Guide governed the accounting and financial reporting for the type of not-for-profit organization within which a particular organization fell. There were separate guides for colleges and universities, voluntary health and welfare organizations, healthcare service providers, and certain other not-for-profit organizations. The reason why this is important is because the SFAS 124 covers many, but not all investments. For the investments not covered by SFAS 124, the not-for-profit would look back to the accounting for investments that was contained in these now-superseded Audit and Accounting Guides. Fortunately, the current AICPA Audit and Accounting Guides for Not-for-Profit and Healthcare Organizations (which now cover all of the not-for-profit organizations formerly covered by the superseded guides) bring forward the otherwise superseded guidance for current use.

Investments in Stocks and Bonds

Those researching accounting principles in SFAS 124 should know that stocks and bonds are referred to by more exacting terms— equities and debt securities—which is the way they will be referred to in this chapter. SFAS 124 established accounting requirements for the following two types of investments:

- All debt securities
- Equity securities with readily determinable market values

SFAS 124 requires that investments in debt securities and investments in equity securities with readily determinable fair values be measured at their fair value in the statement of financial position. For purposes of determining what securities are in its scope, SFAS 124 provides these definitions.

Debt Securities

A debt security is any security representing a creditor relationship with another enterprise. It also includes preferred stock that by its terms either must be redeemed by the issuing enterprise or is redeemable at the option of the investor. In addition, it includes a collateralized mortgage obligation (CMO) or other instrument that is issued in equity form but is required to be accounted for as a nonequity instrument regardless of how that instrument is classified (i.e., whether equity or debt) in the issuer's statement of financial position. However, the definition excludes option contracts, financial futures contracts, lease contracts, and swap contracts.

Equity Securities

An equity security is any security that represents an ownership interest in an enterprise (such as common, preferred, or other capital stock) or the right to acquire an ownership interest (such as warrants, rights, and call options) or to dispose of an ownership interest in an enterprise at fixed or determinable prices (such as put options). However, the term does not include convertible debt or preferred stock that by its terms either must be redeemed by the issuing enterprise or is redeemable at the option of the investor.

Equity securities have readily determinable fair values under SFAS 124 if they meet one of these criteria:

1. Sales prices or bid-and-asked quotations are currently available on a Securities and Exchange Commission (SEC) registered securities exchange (e.g., New York Stock Exchange, American Stock Exchange) or in the over-the-counter mar-

ket, provided the over-the-counter market prices are publicly reported by the National Association of Securities Dealers Automated Quotations (NASDAQ) systems or by the National Quotation Bureau.

2. If traded only on a foreign market, the market is of breadth and scope comparable to one of the U.S. markets referred to in 1 above.

3. If the investment is in a mutual fund, the investor's fair value per share or unit is determined, published, and used as the basis for current transactions.

Equity securities in closely held corporations are unlikely to meet the definition of having a readily determinable fair value. Let us say that a not-for-profit organization owned 10% of the stock of a closely held corporation whose stock *did not* meet any of the three criteria above. If sometime close to the not-for-profit organization's year-end another corporation offers to buy all of the shares of the closely held corporation for $5 million, could the not-for-profit organization conclude that its shares now have a readily determinable fair value of $500,000, or 10% of $5 million? The answer is *no*, because the shares still do not meet any of the criteria. If the sale were consummated, the gain or loss would then be recognized in the financial statement.

Both definitions of debt and equities specifically relate to debt and equity "securities." SFAS 124 defines a security as "a share, participation, or other interest in property of an enterprise of the issuer or an obligation of the issuer that

1. Either is represented by an instrument issued in bearer or registered form or, if not registered by an instrument, is registered in books maintained to record transfers by or on behalf of the issuer,

2. Is of a type commonly dealt in on securities exchanges or markets or, when represented by an instrument, is commonly registered in any area in which it is issued or dealt in as a medium for investment, and

3. Either is one of a class or series or by its terms is divisible

into a class or series of shares, participations, interests or obligations."

Note: One would expect that most ownership interests (i.e., equities)with readily determinable fair values under SFAS's definition will be in the form of a security. The definition of security provided by SFAS 124 is more likely to exclude debts that are not in the form of a security from its scope. For example, a pledge receivable from a donor or an account receivable as a result of a fee-for-service activity is a form of debt payable to a not-for-profit organization, but would not be considered a security using the above definition, so would therefore not be included within the scope of SFAS 124.

Basically, SFAS 124 requires that all debt securities and equity securities with readily determinable market value be reported in the statement of financial position at their fair value. A security's fair value is the amount at which it could be bought or sold in a current transaction between willing parties. Quoted market prices, as described in the three criteria previously outlined, will generally provide the most reliable measure of fair value. As explained, for equity securities, using values as determined in the three criteria is the only way to value the security under SFAS 124 because it must meet the definition of having a readily determinable fair value. Debt securities can be a little more challenging since not every debt security is actively traded on a market. Fortunately for debt securities, however, a fair value can generally be determined by using known fair values of comparable debt securities. To do this, the interest rates, maturities, credit ratings of the issuers, and any special features of the debt securities (such as call provisions) must be taken into account.

To report these securities in the statement of financial position at fair value, one of the more important concepts to understand is what happens to the increase or decrease in fair value from one fiscal year to another. Assuming the security is not sold, these increases or decreases are referred to as unrealized gains or losses. Unrealized gains and losses for each year are reported in the statement of activities for that fiscal year as part of investment income.

When SFAS 124 was first issued by the FASB, this particular feature of the requirements gave many not-for-profits cause for alarm, since changes in the values of their investment portfolios would be reflected in the statement of activities (which, as learned in Chapter 2, is basically their operating statement). Many not-for-profit organizations did not like the fact that temporary changes in the values of investments that they planned to hold for a long period of time would affect their current year's activities statement. As will be described more fully in Chapter 11, not-for-profit organizations usually manage their resources and spending to basically break even every year. Having these uncontrollable fluctuations in the fair values of investments affecting their bottom lines results in frustration for managers of not-for-profit organizations. Nonetheless, the requirements of SFAS 124 are clear, and unrealized gains or losses for the year are to be reflected as part of investment income in the statement of activities. Note that the unrealized gain or loss calculation is performed each year and it is the amount of the change from year to year (and not the cumulative gain or loss) that affects each year's statement of activities. An example should make clear exactly how this works.

Practical Example

Purchase
A not-for-profit organization purchases an investment in a New York Stock Exchange–traded company on August 1, 20X0, at $50 per share. It buys 1,000 shares and incurs a brokerage commission of $1,000, resulting in a total cost of $51,000 ($50 times 1,000, plus the $1,000 transaction fee). It records the amount of the investment as an asset on its statement of financial position at $51,000.

End of First Year
On June 30, 20X1, the fiscal year-end, the quoted market price of the equity security is $61 per share, or $61,000. The not-for-profit organization would report the investment on its statement of financial position at $61,000 and report a $10,000 unrealized gain as part of investment income on its statement of activities.

End of Second Year
On June 30, 20X2, the end of the next fiscal year, the quoted market price of the equity investment is $70 per share, or $70,000. The not-for-profit organization would report the investment at $70,000 on its statement of financial position and report a $9,000 unrealized gain (the difference between $70,000 and $61,000) as part of investment income on its statement of activities. Note that the cumulative amounts reported on the statement activities for the two years ($10,000 plus $9,000) equals the total increase in fair value of the investment ($70,000 less $51,000).

During the Third Year
On March 8, 20X3, the not-for-profit organization sells the investment. It receives a price of $65 per share and pays a $1,000 brokerage commission. The net proceeds from the sale are $65 times 1,000 shares less the $1,000 brokerage commission, which equals $64,000. The not-for-profit organization will report a $6,000 realized loss on the sale of the investment for its fiscal year ending June 30, 20X3, which represents the difference between the carrying amount of $70,000 and the net proceeds from the sale of $64,000. Cumulatively, for as long as the not-for-profit organization owned the investment, it increased in value by $13,000, the difference between its acquisition cost of $51,000 and its net proceeds at the time of sale of $64,000. Similarly, the total of the amounts that were reflected in the statements of activities for the three periods ($10,000 unrealized gain, $9,000 unrealized gain, and a $6,000 realized loss) net to a cumulative gain of $13,000, which is identical to the change in the value of the security for the total time that the not-for-profit organization owned it.

Once the security is sold, a realized gain or loss is recognized in the statement of activities as an increase or a decrease in unrestricted net assets. Realized gains and losses, along with unrealized gains and losses and dividend and interest income, are all reported as part of investment income on the not-for-profit organization's statement of activities. As described above, unrealized gains or losses are reported in the statement of activities as increases or decreases in unrestricted net assets, unless their use is temporarily or permanently restricted either by explicit donor stipulation or by law. Realized and unrealized gains may be offset against realized and unrealized losses on the statement of activities.

Impact of Donor Restrictions

Gains that are limited by donor restrictions may be reported as unrestricted gains if the restrictions are met in the same reporting period and if all of these conditions are met:

- The organization reports similar transactions consistently from period to period.
- The same policy for reporting contributions received is used.
- The accounting policy is disclosed.

A donor-restricted endowment fund is created when a donor stipulates that the contributed assets be invested for a specific period of time or in perpetuity.

Donor stipulations, to the extent that they exist, determine the classifications of gains and losses from sales of restricted endowment funds. Securities held in perpetuity because of donor restrictions also may result in gains or losses increasing or decreasing permanently restricted net assets because of local law.

However, in the absence of donor restrictions or local law that restricts the use of gains, such gains will follow the treatment of investment income. Accordingly, gains are unrestricted if the investment income is unrestricted or are temporarily restricted if the investment income is temporarily restricted by the donor. What happens if the investments of the endowment fund have realized or unrealized losses? SFAS 124 states the following:

> In the absence of donor stipulations or law to the contrary, losses on the investments of a donor-restricted endowment fund shall reduce temporarily restricted net assets to the extent that donor-imposed temporary restrictions on net appre-

ciation of the fund have not been met before the loss occurs. Any remaining loss shall reduce unrestricted net assets.

If losses reduce the assets of a donor-restricted endowment fund below the level required by the donor stipulations or law, gains that restore the fair value of the assets of the endowment fund to the required level shall be classified as increases in unrestricted net assets.

This means that losses on endowment funds that reduce their required level as specified by the donor need to be made up from unrestricted assets.

Tip   Review of the donor stipulations and their effect on investment gains and losses, as well as the effect of local law, may warrant the review of the not-for-profit organization's legal counsel to ensure not only that they are accounted for properly, but also that donor and legal requirements are being complied with.

Investment Income and Expenses

Investment income includes dividends, interest, rents, royalties, and similar payments and should be recognized as earned. The revenue should be reported as an increase in unrestricted, temporarily restricted, or permanently restricted net assets, depending on donor stipulations on the use of the income. For example, if there are no donor-imposed restrictions on the use of the income, it should be reported as an increase in unrestricted net assets.

A donor may stipulate that a gift be invested in perpetuity, with the income to be used to support a specified program. The gift should be recorded as permanently restricted net assets. Investment income that is earned is reported as temporarily restricted. If the restrictions on the income are met, the statement of activities should report a reclassification from temporarily restricted net assets to unrestricted net assets.

Investment expenses may be netted against related investment income, gains, or losses on the statement of activities provided they are disclosed on the statement of activities or in the notes to the financial statements (SFAS 117, para 24).

If the not-for-profit organization presents a statement of functional expenses, investment expenses netted against investment revenue should be reported by their functional classification (*NFP Audit Guide*, para 13.23).

Investments Other than Stocks and Bonds

The AICPA Audit and Accounting Guide for Not-for-Profit Organizations addresses the accounting for "other investments," which are those not-for-profit organization investments that are not covered by SFAS 124. Other investments include, among others, investments in real estate, mortgage notes, venture capital funds, partnership interests, oil and gas interests, and equity securities that have a readily determinable fair value. The longer the endowment portfolio, the more likely it is to include these types of investments. The various superseded AICPA audit and accounting guides monitored earlier in this chapter included guidance concerning other investments. The measurement guidance for accounting for other investments included in these superseded AICPA publications is retained until such time as the FASB or the Accounting Standards Executive Committee (AcSEC) issues more definitive guidance. However, to the extent that the guidance in the superseded AICPA publications requires all investments to be measured using the same measurement attribute, only other investments, rather than all investments, are required to be measured using the same measurement attribute. For example, if a superseded AICPA publication permits investments to be carried at either cost or fair value, provided that the same attribute is used for all investments, and if equity securities with a readily determinable fair value are carried at fair value in conformity with the guidance in SFAS 124, other investments are permitted to be carried at either cost or fair value, provided that the same attribute is used for all other investments.

Specifically the AICPA Audit and Accounting Guide for Not-for-Profit Organizations summarizes the guidance for other investing from the superseded AICPA guides as follows.

Colleges and Universities

Other investments of institutions of higher education, including colleges, universities, and community or junior colleges, that were acquired by purchase may be reported at cost, and contributed other investments may be reported at their fair market value or appraised value at the date of the gift, unless there has been an impairment of value that is not considered to be temporary. Other investments may also be reported at current market value or fair value, provided that the same attribute is used for all other investments. (Investments in wasting assets are usually reported net of an allowance for depreciation or depletion.) The financial statements or notes should set forth the total performance (that is, investment income and realized and unrealized gains and losses) of the investment portfolio.

Voluntary Health and Welfare Organizations

Voluntary health and welfare organizations should report other investments at cost if purchased and at fair market value at the date of the contribution if contributed. If the market value of the other investments portfolio is below the recorded amount, it may be necessary to reduce the carrying amount of the portfolio to market or to provide an allowance for decline in market value. If it can reasonably be expected that the organization will suffer a loss on the disposition of an investment, a provision for the loss should be made in the period in which the decline in value occurs. Carrying other investments at market value is also acceptable. The same measurement attribute should be used for all other investments and should be disclosed.

Other Not-for-Profit Organizations

Not-for-profit organizations (as defined in F ASB Statement 117) that are not colleges, universities, or voluntary health and welfare organizations (that is, those that have been following the Audit and Accounting Guide, Audits of Certain Nonprofit Organizations. and SOP 79-10, Accounting Principles and Reporting Practices for Certain Nonprofit Organizations) should report other investments at either fair value or the lower of cost or fair value. The same measurement attribute should be used for all other investments. Declines in investments carried at the lower of cost or market value should be recognized when their aggregate market value is less than their carrying amount; recoveries of aggregate market value in subsequent periods should be recorded in those periods subject only to the limitation that the carrying amount should not exceed the original cost.

Equity Method of Accounting

The equity method is used by a not-for-profit organization to account for an investment in a company when the not-for-profit organization has the ability to significantly influence that company's financial and operating policies. While all of the details of the equity method are beyond the scope of this book, the non-accountant should be familiar with some of its basic features.

The use of the equity method by a not-for-profit organization is essentially the same as the for-profit sector. When a not-for-profit organization uses the equity method of accounting, its original investment in the investee company is recorded on the statement of financial position at cost. Thereafter, the amount of the investment is adjusted as follows:

- Increased for the organization's proportionate share of the investee company's earnings
- Decreased for the organization's proportionate share of the investee company's losses

- Decreased for dividends received by the not-for-profit organization from the investee company

The statement of financial position should include the investment that the not-for-profit organization has in the for-profit organization. Any earnings and losses from the investee company are reported by the not-for-profit organization on the statement of activities.

The equity method, sometimes referred to as "one-line consolidation," permits the not-for-profit organization to incorporate its pro rata share of the investee company's operating results into its statement of activities. However, rather than include its share of each component (e.g., sales, cost of sales, operating expenses, etc.) in its financial statements, the not-for-profit organization includes its share of the investee's *net* income as a separate line item as an addition (or in the case of a loss, a deduction) to its net assets.

In the absence of evidence to the contrary, an organization is presumed to have the ability to significantly influence an investee company if it owns (directly or indirectly) 20% or more of the investee company's voting stock.

A not-for-profit organization should use the equity method to account for its interest in a for-profit entity if it has the ability to significantly influence the entity's operating and financial policies. However, an organization may choose to report its ownership interest in a for-profit entity at market value if it reports its investment portfolio at market value. In addition, the equity method should not be used to account for an organization's interest in another not-for-profit organization. Instead, the organization should consolidate the investment if it has the ability to control that other organization and it has an economic interest in the related organization.

Ownership percentage determines the accounting method required by the not-for-profit investment in a for-profit entity. When a not-for-profit organization owns less than 20%, the accounting method used to account for the investment is generally fair value, although the rules of SFAS 124 as well as the rules for "other investments" need to be considered. The equity method should be used when the ownership percentage is 20% to 50%. In circumstances where more than 50% of ownership is determined, the for-profit company should be consolidated.

The 20% rule provides some consistency in applying the equity method. An investor's ability to significantly influence an investee depends on a variety of factors and requires evaluation of all circumstances.

For example, if a not-for-profit organization owns less than 20% of the for-profit organization, but does exercise significant influence because of its presence on the board of directors and participation in making policy, the investment should be accounted for under the equity method.

Practical Example   A not-for-profit health-care organization invests $100,000 to obtain 25% of the voting stock of a for-profit company that is developing new types of prosthetic devices for use by disabled individuals. At the end of the for-profit company's fiscal year, it reports net earnings of $10,000. The not-for-profit organization would increase the amount of the investment reported on its statement of financial position by $2,500 (25% of $10,000) to $102,500. At the same time, the not-for-profit organization's statement of activities would report an increase in net assets of $2,500 as income from the investment carried on the equity method of accounting. If, during the year, the for-profit company paid a dividend, the not-for-profit organization would record this dividend as a return of its investment. Let us assume that the total dividend paid was $5,000, of which the not-for-profit organization's 25% share was $1,250. The not-for-profit organization would record the receipt of cash and reduce the amount of the investment recorded on its statement of financial activities by $1,250, so that the investment would be reflected on the organization's statement of financial position at $101,250 ($102,500 less $1,250).

ACCOUNTING AND FINANCIAL REPORTING FOR FINANCIAL INSTRUMENTS

The accounting and financial reporting for financial in-struments is a complex area that usually has a minimal impact for not-for-profit organizations. The purpose of the following discussion is to acquaint the reader with some important terminology and discuss the broad accounting and financial reporting concepts that surround financial instruments. An entire accounting book, literally, could be written about the accounting and disclosure requirements for financial instruments that are going to be described briefly below. Understanding the extent of the complexity of these issues should sufficiently caution the reader against believing that he or she has become an expert in accounting for financial instruments as a result of reading the next few pages.

Perhaps a better term to describe the evolution of accounting standards for financial instruments is *confusing*, rather than *complex*. In the 1990s, several high-visibility institutions incurred major losses as a result of their being party to a type of financial instrument called a *derivative*. The risks associated with derivatives and other financial instruments were thought not to be adequately reflected in what was then the current GAAP for financial statement preparation and disclosure. Accordingly, the FASB acted through several statements to address what it considered necessary disclosures for financial instruments, which resulted in risks that were not readily apparent from the financial statements (so-called off balance sheet risk) as well as concentrations of credit risk that might not be apparent from the financial statements. The major undertaking by the FASB was its project on derivative financial instruments, which addressed more than disclosures in that it addressed how and when derivative financial instruments should be recorded in the statement of financial position and how and when changes in the recorded amounts of derivatives would be reflected in the statements of earnings of commercial enterprises, as well as in the statement of activities for not-for-profit organizations. Once the FASB issued its major statement on accounting for derivatives, FASB Statement No. 133, "Accounting for Derivative Financial Instruments and Hedging Activities" (SFAS 133), some of the previous disclosure requirements became obsolete and were superseded by SFAS 133. For added confusion, the FASB extended the required effective date of SFAS 133 and issued another statement to fine-tune some of the provisions of SFAS 133 that organizations, principally commercial and financial organizations, were having difficulty implementing.

When all of the dust settles from this churning of accounting requirements, what is left for a not-for-profit organization to deal with? Basically, for all financial instruments, which will be defined below, there are some disclosure requirements as to the fair value of these financial instruments, as well as concentrations of credit risk relating to these instruments. In addition, if the not-for-profit organization is a party to a type of financial instrument known as a derivative or participates in hedging activities, the rules for recording these transactions in the financial statements as a result of SFAS 133 must be followed. Following this simplistic breakdown, the next few pages describe the broad requirements for each of these main requirements.

Disclosures about Fair Values of Financial Instruments

Financial instruments are defined in FASB Statement No. 107, "Disclosures about Fair Value of Financial Instruments" (SFAS 107), as follows: "A financial instrument is defined as cash, evidence of an ownership interest in an entity, or a contract that both:

   a. Imposes on one entity a contractual obligation
     (1) to deliver cash or another financial instrument to a second entity or
     (2) to exchange other financial instruments on potentially unfavorable terms with a second entity.
   b. Conveys to that second entity a contractual right
     (1) to receive cash or another financial instrument from the first entity or

(2) to exchange other financial instruments on potentially favorable terms with the first entity."

Reader caution: Before thinking, "Well, I don't think that the soccer club whose board I sit on has any of these, so I'll skip the rest of this chapter," please read on.

Using the above definition, these would be considered financial instruments:

- Cash and short-term investments
- Contributions receivable
- Accounts receivable
- Long-term investments
- Loans receivable
- Accounts payable
- Long-term debt

What is common in these assets and liabilities is the contractual right to receive or pay cash. This definition means that basically the financial assets and liabilities of not-for-profit organizations would meet the definition of a financial instrument so that these disclosure requirements need to be considered.

This paragraph, admittedly, may cause some readers to skip to the credit risk concentration section. These fair value disclosures are optional for certain nonpublic entities that meet each of these criteria:

- The entity is a nonpublic entity. This basically means that the organization does not have its stock or debt publicly traded and is not subject to the reporting requirements of the U.S. Securities and Exchange Commission.
- The entity's total assets are less than $100 million on the date of the financial statements.
- The entity has no instrument, in whole or part, that is accounted for as a derivative financial instrument. (See the discussion later in this chapter for determining whether this requirement is met.)

If the not-for-profit organization does not qualify for exemption of the disclosure requirements of SFAS 107 as listed above, it will need to disclose the fair values and the carrying amounts (that is, the amounts that these financial instruments are reported at in the statement of financial position). This disclosure is usually contained in the notes to the financial statements. Most of a not-for-profit organization's investments are already carried in the statement of financial position at fair value, and in the case of most ordinary, short-term receivables and payables, the carrying amount approximates the fair value. Complying with the disclosure items for these types of amounts should be relatively easy. Determining a fair value for financial instruments, such as long-term debt, will require more effort.

Some financial instruments, such as commitments to extend credit, standby letters of credit, and written financial guarantees are not financial instruments that are recognized in the financial statements, but fall under the fair value disclosure requirements of SFAS 107 and should not be overlooked in preparing the required disclosures.

Disclosures about Concentrations of Credit Risk for All Financial Instruments

There is no exception to these requirements for certain nonpublic entities, so all not-for-profit organizations should comply with these requirements, which are based on the requirements of SFAS 133. In brief, the following disclosures are required when there is credit risk that is concentrated in one or a group of counterparties to a financial instrument:

- Information about the shared region, activity, or economic characteristic that identifies the concentration
- Maximum amount of credit loss that would be incurred if the counterparties failed
- Organization's policy for requiring collateral to support financial instruments that are subject to credit risk

- Organization's policy for entering into netting agreements that seek to minimize credit risk

These disclosures may sound obscure and unrelated to the environment of not-for-profit organizations, but here are two concrete examples as to why these types of disclosures might be important for the financial statement reader:

- *A not-for-profit organization maintains checking and time deposit accounts in several local banks that each exceeds the $100,000 FDIC limit.* The not-for-profit is at risk for the uninsured amounts if these banks fail, and this risk is concentrated in small banks in the same economic region.
- *A not-for-profit organization has focused all of its fund-raising activities on recently minted "dot.com millionaires."* A large percentage of the organization's contributions receivable are from these individuals, which, while still expected to be collected, are concentrated in a group that may experience financial difficulties in the future.

Keep in mind that the disclosure requirements are not centered around the fact that banks do indeed fail and that donors do not always pay their pledges, but are focused on when that credit risk is higher to the organization because it is concentrated in counterparties (in the above example, banks or donors) that have similar characteristics. In this case, the size and location of the banks and the economic activities of the donor serve to concentrate the risk for these financial instruments.

Accounting for Derivatives and Hedging Activities

Derivatives are financial instruments whose value is derived from something else. For example, the value of a stock purchase (call) option or sale (put) option is derived from the value of the underlying stock. The value of a foreign currency future will fluctuate with the value of that foreign currency. The current value of a commodity contract (buying or selling a predetermined amount of wheat, natural gas, corn, fuel oil, etc., at a future point in time for a predetermined price) will be derived from the current price of wheat, natural gas, corn, fuel oil, and so on.

To avoid oversimplifying what is included in the definition of derivatives, here is how they are specifically defined by SFAS 133.

SFAS 133 defines a derivative instrument as a financial instrument or other contract with all three of the following characteristics:

1. It has (a) one or more "underlyings" and (b) one or more "notional amounts" or payment provisions or both. These terms determine the amount of the settlement(s) and whether or not a settlement is required. An underlying is a specified interest rate, security price, commodity price, foreign exchange rate, index of prices or other rates, or other variable. A notional amount is a number of currency units, shares, bushels, pounds, or other units specified in a contract.

2. It requires no initial net investment or an initial net investment that is smaller than would be required for other types of contracts that would be expected to have a similar response to changes in market factors.

3. Its terms require or permit net settlement, it can readily be settled by a means outside the contract, or it provides for delivery of an asset that puts the recipient in a position not substantially different from net settlement.

The best way to understand this definition is to take one or two of the above examples and see how its characteristics match the three components of the definition.

SFAS 133 has two main accounting components. First, it requires that derivatives be recognized as either assets or liabilities in the statement of financial position and that they be measured at fair value. Second, it specifies the accounting for changes in the fair values of derivatives, that is, unrealized gains and losses.

On the first component, not-for-profit organizations would

follow the requirements of SFAS 133 as would commercial enterprises (albeit not-for-profit organizations are far less likely to have derivative instruments to record as assets and liabilities than are commercial enterprises, particularly financial institutions).

On the second component, SFAS 133 provides very specific guidance for determining when derivatives are considered one of several types of hedges—the importance of which is whether changes in the fair values of derivatives are reflected in earnings of the current period or whether these changes are reported not in earnings, but as a component of comprehensive income. For not-for-profit organizations, determination of whether a derivative qualifies as a particular type of hedge is basically irrelevant, since not-for-profit organizations do not report comprehensive income. They only report increases and decreases in net assets in a statement of activities. Accordingly, except for special rules that apply to hedges of exposure to a net investment in a foreign operation, which is discussed later in this section, not-for-profit organizations would report all changes in the fair values of derivative instruments that are recorded as assets or liabilities in their statements of activities as increases or decreases in net assets.

However, if the hedging instrument is designated as a hedge of the foreign currency exposure of a net investment in a foreign operation, then the hedge is reported in the same manner as a translation adjustment to the extent it is effective as a hedge in a manner that is consistent with accounting for foreign currency translation, which is beyond the scope of this book. Suffice it to say that the SFAS 133 provisions for recognizing the gain or loss on assets designated as being hedged in a fair value hedge do not apply to the hedge of a net investment in a foreign operation.

Disclosure Requirements

The disclosure requirements of SFAS 133 relating to not-for-profit organizations that hold or issue derivative instruments would relate to those derivative instruments designated as hedges of the foreign currency exposure of a net investment in a foreign operation. The disclosures would consist of the organization's objectives for holding or issuing those instruments, the context needed to understand those objectives, and the organization's strategies for achieving those objectives. For other derivative instruments, the description should include the purpose of the derivative activity. Gains or losses included in the statement of activities relating to changes in the fair value of derivative instruments would also be disclosed, if not evident from the statement of activities.

SUMMARY

As can be learned from this chapter, the requirements of GAAP relative to investments and financial instruments grow in complexity as types of investments and other financial instruments held by a not-for-profit organization grow in variety and complexity. The reader should keep focused on the fact that most investments are reported in the statement of financial position at fair value and changes in fair value from one year to the next are reported as increases or decreases in the statement of activities. All of the other variations discussed in this chapter are essentially interpretations or occasional exceptions to this general rule.

CHAPTER 5

Accounting for Activities with Joint Costs and Indirect Cost Allocation

This chapter addresses the accounting for situations where a cost incurred by a not-for-profit organization relates to two different activities. There are really two very different topics imbedded in the concepts that will be presented in this chapter.

The first topic to be covered concerns specific rules that are part of GAAP that pertain to situations where an informational activity undertaken by a not-for-profit organization contains a fund-raising appeal. Should the costs incurred in this activity be treated as a program activity or as a fund-raising activity?

The second topic concerns the broad area of indirect cost allocation by not-for-profit organizations. While there really is no specific GAAP relating to indirect cost allocation plans used by not-for-profit organizations, many organizations employ some system to determine the full costs of their program activi-ties. These cost allocation plans result in amounts that are reflected in the financial statements, with a particular impact on the functional reporting in the statement of activities, so a financial statement reader should have an understanding of how these plans work.

ACCOUNTING FOR THE COSTS OF ACTIVITIES
THAT INCLUDE FUND-RAISING

As extensively covered in Chapter 2, not-for-profit organizations report their expenses in functional classifications. You may recall that expenses related to activities are segregated into these functional classifications:

- Program activities
- Supporting services, which include:
  - Management and general
  - Fund-raising
  - Membership development (for membership organizations)

The proportion of expenses that relate to program activities to total expenses and the proportion of expenses that relate to supporting services to total expenses are important performance indicators for not-for-profit organizations. These percentages might indicate to a donor, for example, that for every dollar contributed to the not-for-profit organization, 80 cents is spent on program activities and 20 cents is spent on supporting services. Theoretically, a donor would look more kindly on this organization than one that spends 60 cents of every dollar on program activities and 40 cents on supporting services. Donors, for the most part, want their contributions to go toward program activities, not supporting activities, since that is usually why they contribute to a particular organization.

In addition, not-for-profit organizations generally do not like to show that they spend a high percentage of their expenses on fund-raising. This is another performance indicator. Comparing total contributions to fund-raising expenses gives a donor an indication of how much of each dollar raised is spent on fund-raising, which, as part of supporting services, is not usually the primary reason why a donor contributes to a particular not-for-profit organization.

Chapter 11 provides additional discussion of the financial indicators that are important to understanding a not-for-profit organization's financial statements.

All of this is important because it provides the reason that there are specific rules in GAAP for allocating a particular type of cost that includes a fund-raising appeal. The specific rules are created by the AICPA Statement of Position No. 98-2, "Accounting for Costs of Activities of Not-for-Profit Organizations and State and Local Governmental Entities That Include Fund-Raising" (SOP 98-2). Prior to the issuance of SOP 98-2, the rules for determining when the costs of activities that include fund-raising could be allocated to functions other than fund-raising were somewhat weak and some not-for-profit organizations probably erred on the side of allocating too many costs out of fund-raising expenses and into program activity expenses. To make sure that costs are allocated only in appropriate circumstances, SOP 98-2 sets up hurdles (it calls them criteria) that must be cleared before costs can be allocated. Once it is determined that costs can be allocated, SOP 98-2 provides guidance for how to allocate those costs.

Note also that SOP 98-2 only covers those costs that include fund-raising activities. Accordingly, it covers activities that may be part fund-raising and part program, management, and general or membership development. It does not cover activities that are part of two activities other than fund-raising, such as part program and part management and general.

Let us first discuss the criteria that must be met and then discuss allocation techniques.

Criteria Permitting Cost Allocation

It is important to note that the not-for-profit organization must meet the criteria established by SOP 98-2 before any costs can be allocated. If the criteria are not met, the entire cost of the activity is classified as a fund-raising activity. For example, consider a mailing being prepared by a not-for-profit organization that is part program activity and part fund-raising. If one of the criteria is not met, all of the costs of the mailing are recorded as fund-raising expenses, despite its being clear that there is some program material included in the mailing.

Tip   Not-for-profit organizations do not develop their program and fund-raising mailings in a vacuum. Obviously, it is important that the not-for-profit be familiar with the criteria of SOP 98-2 so that none of its actions would preclude any of the criteria being met and thereby preclude any cost allocation.

The three criteria prescribed by SOP 98-2, whose specific requirements are to be described in more detail, are:

- Purpose criterion
- Audience criterion
- Content criterion

Purpose Criterion

The purpose criterion is the most extensive and difficult to apply of the three criteria. It is met if the purpose of the joint activity that includes fund-raising also includes accomplishing program or management and general functions.

Program functions.   Only activities that include program activities would need to meet this portion of the purpose criterion test. In order for the purpose to accomplish program functions, the activity should call for specific action by the audience that will help accomplish the entity's mission. (For example, if the not-for-profit organization's mission is to reduce the risk of heart attacks, an activity that motivates an audience to take action would be one that calls on the audience to lose weight, exercise, eat healthy, etc., by suggesting ways that the audience could accomplish this.)

For program functions, if this test is met, then the test in the following section is applied. (For management and general activities, only the test in the following section is applied.)

Program functions and management and general functions.   Both program functions and management and general functions would need to pass certain tests in order to meet the purpose criterion. SOP 98-2 specifies these factors that should be considered in the order in which they are listed to determine if the purpose criterion is met:

1. *Whether compensation or fees for performing the activity are based on contributions raised.* The purpose criterion is automatically failed if a majority of the compensation or fees for any party's performance of any component of the discrete joint activity varies based on contributions raised for that discrete joint activity. In other words, if this activity is performed by a consultant whose fees are based on the amount of compensation raised, then the test would be failed.

2. *Whether similar program or management and general activity is conducted separately and on a similar or greater scale.* This test determines whether the program or management and general activities have enough substance that they are conducted at other times even if there is no fund-raising appeal included. The purpose criterion is met if either of these two conditions is met:

Condition 1
- The program component of the joint activity calls for specific action by the recipient that will help accomplish the entity's mission, and
- A similar program component is conducted without the fund-raising component using the same medium and on a scale that is similar to or greater than the scale on which it is conducted with the fund-raising.

Condition 2
- A management and general activity that is similar to the management and general component of the joint activ-

ity being accounted for is conducted without the fund-raising component using the same medium and on a scale that is similar to or greater than the scale on which it is conducted without fund-raising.

3. *Other evidence.* If the factors described in 1 or 2 do not determine whether the purpose criterion is met, other evidence may be used to determine this. All available evidence, both positive and negative, should be considered to determine whether the purpose criterion is met. SOP 98-2 provides examples of indicators that provide evidence for making this determination.

For example, evidence that the purpose criterion may be met includes:

- The entity measures the program results and accomplishments of the joint activity.
- The activity has a call to action by the recipient that will accomplish the entity's mission, and if the entity conducts the program component with a significant fund-raising component in a different medium.

Evidence that the purpose criterion may not be met includes:

- The evaluation of any party's involved performance for the joint activity is based on the contributions raised, or whether some, but less than a majority, of compensation or fees for any party's performance of any component of the joint activity varies based on contributions raised for the discrete joint activity.

The not-for-profit organization may evaluate both the program results as well as the fund-raising results of a joint activity. The relative weight that the organization gives to each of the evaluation results may be indicative of whether the purpose criterion has been met.

Other evidence may also be provided by the qualifications of the consultants or the employees that perform the joint activity. For example, if the joint activity is handled exclusively by a consultant that performs fund-raising activities, this evidence may suggest that the purpose criterion has not been met. On the other hand, if the joint activity is handled almost exclusively by employees who work on program activities (and are not members of the fund-raising department), evidence is provided that the purpose criterion may be met.

SOP 98-2 also provides a list of tangible evidence of intent that may assist an organization in determining whether the purpose criterion is met. Examples include:

1. The organization's written mission statement, as stated on its fund-raising activities, bylaws, or annual report.
2. Minutes of board of directors' (and committee) meetings or other meetings.
3. Restrictions imposed by donors (who are not related parties) on gifts intended to fund the related parties.
4. Long-range plans or operating activities.
5. Written instructions to other entities, such as scriptwriters, consultants, or list brokers, concerning the purpose of the joint activity.
6. Internal management memoranda.

Note: A not-for-profit organization does not need to meet 1 or 2 above to meet the purpose criterion. If 1 is not met then 2 is considered. If 2 is not met then 3 is considered. The application of the various forms of evidence described above that are considered as part of the "other evidence" will clearly require significant judgment on the part of the financial statement preparer. Not-for-profit organizations are likely to become more sensitive to how they characterize joint activities (particularly in some of the tangible evidence forms described above) so that if their intention or purpose is to accomplish program or management and general functions, that intention or purpose will not be overshadowed by inadvertent evidence which indicates that the purpose criterion has not been met.

Audience Criterion

The substance of these criteria is that it would be hard to justify an activity as partially program or management and general if the target audience is basically selected because they have contributed to the not-for-profit organization in the past. SOP 98-2 presumes that the audience criterion is not met if the audience of a joint activity includes prior donors or is otherwise selected based on its ability or likelihood to contribute to the not-for-profit organization. However, this presumption can be overcome if the audience is also selected for one or more of these reasons:

1. The audience's need to use or reasonable potential for use of the specific action called for by the program component of the joint activity.
2. The audience's ability to take specific action to assist the entity in meeting the goals of the program component of the joint activity.
3. The not-for-profit organization is required to direct the management and general component of the joint activity to the particular audience or the audience has reasonable potential for use of the management and general component.

If the audience does not contain prior donors, or is not otherwise selected based on its ability or likelihood to contribute, the audience criterion is met if the audience is selected for one or more of the above reasons.

Content Criterion

The content criterion is met if the joint activity supports program or management and general functions as follows:

1. *Program.* The joint activity calls for specific action by the recipient that will help accomplish the organization's mission.
2. *Management and general.* The joint activity fulfills one or

more of the organization's management and general responsibilities through a component of the joint activity.

The content criterion is fairly general since the AICPA was not interested in getting involved in determining the content of not-for-profit organizations' materials. It is probably the easiest of the criteria for organizations to meet.

ALLOCATION METHODS

Once a not-for-profit organization meets the criteria previously described and determines that it is able to allocate costs between fund-raising activities and program activities or management and general activities, the next task to be undertaken is to determine how the cost allocation is actually going to be accomplished.

First, it is important to understand that some of the costs that may be allocated between fund-raising and program or management and general activities may actually be directly identifiable. For example, assume that a mailing that meets all of the criteria includes a printed booklet that is solely a program activity and is accompanied by a second booklet that includes a fund-raising appeal along with a business reply envelope in which to mail a contribution. The cost of producing and printing the program booklet is a direct expense of a program activity and the cost of the fund-raising appeal booklet and the business reply envelope is a direct fund-raising activity. These costs do not have to be allocated—they can be determined separately.

Caution Just to reiterate, if one of the criteria is not met, the entire cost of this mailing, including the program booklet, would be charged to fund-raising expenses.

The costs to be allocated in this example are likely to be the costs of the envelope and the postage. SOP 98-2 requires that the cost allocation method used to allocate these types of costs be "rational and systematic," resulting in an allocation of costs that is reasonable. There are many different ways that costs such as these can be allocated. Three methods that are provided as examples in SOP 98-2 would be representative and illustrative of methods that could be used. These methods are:

- *Physical units method.* This method allocates costs based on the physical materials that make up the joint costs. In the above example, postage would be allocated based on the relative weights of the program booklet and the fundraising booklet to the total weight of each piece of the mailing. The number of lines or the number of pages in each document might also be used.

- *Relative direct method.* This method allocates joint costs in relation to the direct costs of each of the activities. In this example, the direct cost of each of the booklets would be determined and the postage would be allocated based on the percentage of each to the total. For example, if the program booklet costs $7,000 to produce and the fund-raising booklet costs $3,000 to produce, then 70% of the postage ($7,000 divided by $10,000) would be allocated to program activities and 30% ($3,000 divided by $10,000) of the postage would be allocated to fund-raising activities.

- *Stand-alone cost method.* This method allocates joint costs to each component of the joint activity on a ratio that estimates the costs that would have been incurred had the joint activity been performed separately. In this example, let us say that the program booklet would have cost $3 per piece to mail separately and the fund-raising booklet would have cost $2 per piece to mail. Together, in the same envelope, the mailing cost is $4. The stand-alone cost of the program activity relative to the total cost would be $3 divided by $5 ($3 plus $2) or 60%. The cost allocated to program activities would be 60% of the mailing cost of $4, or $2.40 per piece. The cost allocated to fund-raising would be 40% ($2 divided by $3 plus $2) of $4, or $1.60 per piece. Of course, this calculation could also be done relative to the stand-alone costs of the entire mailing (that is, how much it would cost to mail all of the pieces, instead of individual pieces).

While there are more details contained in SOP 98-2 as to allocating joint costs, the above discussion should give the non-accountant more than enough information to understand the importance of these allocations, when the allocations can be made, and some of the allocation methodologies that can be used. SOP 98-2 contains 17 illustrative examples of the application of the criteria and allocation methodologies that can be of use to not-for-profit organizations and their independent auditors in dealing with those instances when it is not readily determinable if the criteria have been met. While the criteria described above may seem very specific, applying them to the wide variety of circumstances that are encountered in the everyday activities of not-for-profit organizations can make them seem less than clear-cut.

INDIRECT COST ALLOCATION PLANS

As stated above, SOP 98-2 covers a very specific area of cost allocation that involves fund-raising activities. There are many other times, however, when not-for-profit organizations allocate costs, and that will be the topic of the pages that follow. In order to report expenses in their functional classifications—program expenses, management and general expenses, fund-raising expenses, and, if applicable, membership development expenses—a methodology to allocate indirect costs is often needed. In addition, not-for-profit organizations provide program services under contracts or grants that provide for reimbursement of the organization for costs incurred. In order to recover both direct and indirect expenses, a not-for-profit organization needs a way to allocate indirect costs to specific programs so that they can be recovered along with the direct costs of the program. The costs that usually need to be allocated are those that are referred to as indirect costs. Sometimes not-for-profit organizations have a formal indirect cost allocation plan that calculates the rate at which they charge indirect costs to particular activities. Often these indirect cost allocation plans are developed when a not-for-profit organization has contracts or grants that are provided by another entity, often a government, on a cost-reimbursement basis. Indirect cost allocation assures that not-for-profit organizations are reimbursed for the total costs under the contract or grant, which include indirect costs.

Before getting too far into the details, however, it is important to understand the distinction between direct costs and indirect costs. Direct costs are those expenses that can be specifically attributed to a particular activity. Direct costs can include various types of expenses, such as salaries, supplies, and subcontractor payments. Indirect costs are all of the expenses that are *not* direct expenses. Many organizations consider rent, utilities, and independent audit costs to be part of their indirect costs. These definitions are intentionally general, which is important to understand, because organizations can choose to set up indirect cost allocation plans in a variety of different ways to satisfy their own needs. There are no specific principles in GAAP that would dictate how an indirect cost allocation plan should be set up. In preparing the financial statements in accordance with GAAP, it would be required to maintain consistency in the application of indirect cost allocation plans, particularly as these plans result in amounts that impact the financial statements. As mentioned earlier, many times these plans are developed in response to the need for a cost allocation methodology to determine the whole cost of a program administered under a particular contract or grant. As long as the indirect cost allocation is acceptable to the other party to the contract or grant (that is, the party that will be reimbursing the not-for-profit organization for the costs incurred under contract or grant) and there is consistency and reasonableness in the approach, a great variety of methods can be developed and used. One caution, however, is that to the extent that the indirect cost allocation plan is used under contract or grant administered under a federal program, there are specific federal cost requirements that need to be adhered to in order for the indirect cost allocation plan to be acceptable to the federal agency that is administering the particular award or contract. While the specific federal requirements are beyond the scope

of this book, it is important for readers to be aware of these requirements in case they are involved with a not-for-profit organization that is the recipient of a federal award program.

One of the problems in trying to explain how indirect cost
allocation plans work is that the plans can vary widely from one
organization to another, even in those organizations that are required to follow the federal guidelines described above. Exhibit
5.1 demonstrates the basic techniques that can be used, and where
applicable, different options that might be used are explained.

The first step in developing an indirect cost allocation plan is
to determine what will be considered indirect costs. These costs
should be those that are not readily attributable to a particular
activity or function of the not-for-profit organization. For example,
the organization's costs of maintaining its executive office person-
nel, accounting staff, and legal counsel are often considered part
of the pool of costs that are considered indirect costs. On the other

EXHIBIT 5.1   Indirect cost allocation methodology

Direct costs

	Program A	Program B	Total
Salaries	$335,000	$265,000	$600,000
Materials	$15,000	$25,000	$40,000
Subcontractor payments	$400,000	$500,000	$900,000
Total	$750,000	$790,000	$1,540,000

Indirect costs

Salaries and fringe benefits	
Executive director	$150,000
Accounting staff	$50,000
Administrative staff	$40,000
	$240,000
Rent and utilities	$15,000
Supplies and other office expenses	$45,000
	$300,000

hand, the organization's costs of maintaining staff assigned to a specific program activity would generally be considered a direct cost of that activity. Rent or occupancy costs are most often considered part of indirect costs. However, if specific staff are assigned to a particular program or activity, and the rent costs for the portion of the total office that is used by this staff can be identified, this portion of the total rent expense might be considered a direct cost of the program or activity.

As a very simplistic example, consider the indirect cost allocation methodology in Exhibit 5.1. Since the actual costs will not be known until after the fiscal year is completed, usually an estimate of an indirect cost rate is used for planning purposes by using either the prior year's actual expense amounts or the current year's budgeted information.

Total direct costs equal $1,540,000 and total indirect costs equal $300,000. The next step is to choose a basis over which to allocate the indirect costs. This particular sample organization determines that salary costs directly charged to program activities is a reasonable basis to use to allocate its indirect costs. In this case, an indirect cost rate is calculated by dividing the total of the indirect costs ($300,000) by the basis over which it is to be allocated ($600,000), which results in an indirect cost rate of 50%. Therefore, for every dollar of salary costs directly charged to a program, the organization will tack on an overhead charge equal to 50% of the direct salary costs.

Let us say that another organization with the same set of facts decides to use total direct program costs as the basis over which to allocate indirect costs. In this case, an indirect cost rate is calculated by dividing the total of the indirect costs ($300,000) by the basis over which it is to be allocated ($1,540,000), which results in an indirect cost rate of 19.5%. Therefore, for every dollar of program costs directly charged to a program, the organization will tack on an overhead charge equal to 19.5% of the direct program costs.

As can be seen from this very simple example, the indirect cost rate calculated by a not-for-profit organization varies significantly depending on what basis the organization uses to allocate the indirect costs. While the first calculation results in an indirect cost rate of 50%, the second calculation is far less at 19.5%. On the surface, the second calculation would seem to indicate that the organization is far more efficient than an organization that uses the first method. In actuality, although the percentages differ greatly, they reflect the exact same set of financial information. The difference is solely in the selection of the basis on which to allocate the indirect costs.

Here are some other differences that could impact the actual rate calculated as a not-for-profit organization's indirect cost rate:

- An accountant in an accounting department spends all of his or her time preparing financial reports for one particular program. One not-for-profit organization may choose to charge the cost of this accountant directly to the program. Another organization might treat this cost as part of its indirect costs.

- The salary costs of an executive director of a not-for-profit organization may be treated fully as an indirect cost. Another organization might determine by analyzing the executive director's time sheets or other records that he or she spends 20% of their time on Program A, 20% on Program B, 20% on fund-raising, and the remaining 40% on general organization matters. Each program would be charged 20% of the executive director's salary costs. The fund-raising activity would be charged 20% of the executive director's salary costs. The remaining 40% of the executive director's salary costs would be treated as indirect costs.

- A not-for-profit organization might treat all telephone costs as an indirect cost. Another organization might have staff keep track of long-distance calls made for a particular activity and treat these as direct costs. The remaining telephone costs would be treated as indirect costs.

Suffice it to say that there are many ways to construct indirect cost allocation plans as a means to accumulate total costs for programs and other activities. To the extent that these plans are used to charge costs to cost-reimbursable contracts or grants, there are several cautions that should be considered by not-for-profit organizations. First, these contracts or grants may specify that the not-for-profit organization will be reimbursed only for certain types of direct expenses. Irrespective of the not-for-profit organization's indirect cost allocation plan, only those costs allowable under the grant or contract will be reimbursed. It is key to keep these specific provisions in mind when the organization calculates its indirect cost rate and uses this rate for planning purposes. Assuming that certain costs will be reimbursed when they actually will *not* be reimbursed can have a very detrimental effect on the finances of a not-for-profit organization. Second, some contracts or grants either cap the rate at which they will reimburse indirect costs or specify an indirect cost rate that will be reimbursed. Again, the not-for-profit organization has to be aware of these limitations in formulating an indirect cost allocation plan, because the plan should not anticipate that indirect costs will be reimbursed at the calculated indirect cost rate since, in some cases, they may not be.

A final word about indirect cost allocation plans involves consistency. Regardless of whether the indirect cost rate is used to allocate costs among program, management and general, and fund-raising for the purpose of function reporting in the statement of activities or for calculating costs to be charged to a cost-reimbursement contract or grant, the not-for-profit organization must be consistent in how it treats particular types of costs. While there is a great disparity in practice as to how indirect cost allocation plans work, a not-for-profit organization must define its methodology and apply it consistently. The application of the plan often involves others besides accounting staff. For example, if an organization chooses to identify long-distance telephone charges and treat these costs as a direct expense, the individuals actually making the telephone calls must not only know that they need to keep track of the purpose of their calls but also know how to communicate this information to the appropriate accounting staff member who is given the responsibility for calculating direct telephone costs.

SUMMARY

Not-for-profit organizations must present functional expense information on their statement of activities, reflecting program, management and general, and fund-raising expenses. GAAP has some specific cost allocation rules as to when and how the costs of activities that include fund-raising may be allocated. In addition, many not-for-profit organizations develop indirect cost allocation plans not only in order to allocate costs to particular functions, but also to determine the full costs of individual programs, particularly those that result in the reimbursement to the not-for-profit organization for actual costs incurred.

CHAPTER 6

Affiliated Organizations

A discussion of not-for-profit organizations that are affiliated organizations is difficult because there are so many different types of affiliations between and among not-for-profit organizations. The basic accounting rules attempt to provide guidance for all types and variations of these affiliations. This chapter will discuss the basic rules under GAAP that will assist the reader in understanding the potential impacts on financial statements that can occur when a reporting not-for-profit organization has other not-for-profit organizations that are considered to be affiliated with the reporting not-for-profit organization for financial reporting purposes. While Chapter 3 discusses the accounting for the situation where an affiliate raises funds on behalf of other organizations and passes those funds through to the recipient organizations, this chapter discusses the question of whether affiliated organizations are so closely related their financial statements should be consolidated into a single presentation.

This chapter will also discuss the impact on financial statements of a not-for-profit organization when it has a for-profit subsidiary. Also, in this chapter is a discussion of what are considered related parties under GAAP and how transactions between a not-for-profit organization and a related party are reflected in the financial statements of a not-for-profit organization.

AFFILIATED ORGANIZATIONS

The different types of affiliations between and among not-for-profit organizations are varied and many. For example, the following types of associations or affiliations may be encountered in the environment of not-for-profit organizations:

- An organization, "Friends of the Zoo," may raise funds that are used for programs or other activities that enhance the activities of a not-for-profit organization that operates a zoo. The Friends of the Zoo may accept contributions, which it is required to pass through to the zoo. On the other hand, it may accept other contributions that it either uses for its own operations or has the discretion to decide are to be used by the zoo or for some other related purpose. As described in Chapter 3, this example (as well as some of the following examples, depending on the actual nature of the contributions) may result in questions about when both or either of these organizations would report the receipt of assets as contributions revenue on their own financial statements. This question is somewhat different from determining whether the financial statements of the Friends of the Zoo, and the other applicable examples, should be combined with those of the zoo (and the other organizations in the examples that follow).
- A college alumni association may not only raise funds for the college or university but may also conduct a wide variety of activities for the alumni on its own behalf.
- A hospital auxiliary may raise funds that are used for hospital-related activities. In this case, raising funds from an organization legally independent from the hospital may permit the hospital some flexibility in the use of the funds as opposed to those expenditures more strictly controlled from such requirements of Medicare or Medicaid, for example.
- Large donor-restricted endowment funds may be placed in a separate legal entity. In addition, if the not-for-profit

organization has obtained more assets than it currently needs, it may decide to place those assets in a separate legal entity. Prospective donors to a not-for-profit organization are generally not pleased to see that the not-for-profit organization itself has more money than it needs, so "parking" these funds in another entity sometimes solves this appearance problem.

- A social services organization sets up separate legal entities to handle its senior-citizens programs, its prenatal care programs, and its day-care services.
- A university sets up separate legal entities to handle its food service function, parking facility function, and bookstore.
- A national professional accounting organization establishes separate chapters in major cities, with each chapter being a separate legal entity.

Accounting for Not-for-Profit Affiliated Organizations

There are specific rules in GAAP which determine whether the financial statements of affiliated organizations should be combined and presented as if the affiliated organizations were one organization. These rules are promulgated by AICPA Statement of Position No. 94-3, "Reporting of Related Entities by Not-for-Profit Organizations" (SOP 94-3).

Tip   The Financial Accounting Standards Board has recently revised the rules for accounting for business combinations. As a separate subproject of that effort, the FASB is reviewing the requirements and methodology for consolidations of financial statements of not-for-profit organizations. This project, which has not yet been completed, is discussed in Chapter 12, which covers upcoming accounting developments that are likely to affect not-for-profit organizations. It may be confusing for some to distinguish between business combinations and the preparation of consolidated financial statements. Business combinations basically deal with how transactions that result in the combination or change in ownership of two separate organizations are accounted for and reported in financial statements prepared in accordance with GAAP. Consolidation of financial statements occurs in financial reporting periods after the date of a business combination (or other similar event that causes consolidated financial statements to be required) and in subsequent periods. Consolidation is basically the ongoing accounting that occurs after the initial accounting for a business combination.

SOP 94-3 describes the accounting by not-for-profit organizations for investments in for-profit subsidiaries. This guidance is discussed later in this chapter. However, the most significant guidance provided by SOP 94-3 for not-for-profit organizations relates to the accounting and financial reporting for not-for-profit organizations that are financially interrelated.

In most cases, not-for-profit organizations don't have voting ownership shares that may be purchased or acquired by other not-for-profit organizations. Accordingly, the rules applicable to whether to consolidate one not-for-profit organization with another are not as straightforward as with for-profit investments and subsidiaries that are described later in this chapter. How not-for-profit organizations that are financially interrelated combine, consolidate, or account for their relationship is based on three concepts described by SOP 94-3 as:

- Ownership
- Control
- Economic interest

Ownership

Ownership interest in not-for-profit organizations may be evidenced in a variety of ways because a not-for-profit organization may have one of many different legal forms. For example, not-for-profit organizations may be in the legal form of corporations issuing stock, corporations issuing ownership certificates, membership corporations issuing membership certificates, joint ventures, partnerships, and other forms.

Control

Control is the direct or indirect ability to determine the direction of management and policies through ownership, contract, or otherwise. In evaluating whether one not-for-profit organization controls another, factors such as these should be taken into consideration:

- Control of one organization by another might be clearly indicated in the organizational relationship of the two organizations as described in legal documents and other publications. For example, one not-for-profit organization's charter, bylaws, or articles of incorporation may indicate that it is controlled by another not-for-profit organization. Similarly, other less formal documents, such as annual reports, grant proposals, and fund-raising brochures, may provide an indication of control of one organization by another.
- The board of one not-for-profit organization may be appointed by the board of another not-for-profit organization, providing a clear indication of control. Less clear, but still compelling as indications of control are when one not-for-profit organization's board either approves the selection of board members of another organization or needs to ratify the major decisions of the other organization's board of directors or management.
- One not-for-profit organization must approve the budget of the other not-for-profit organization.

The determination of control must be made on an individual basis and the above factors are neither a complete list, nor meant to be absolutely conclusive as to whether criteria for control of one not-for-profit organization by another for purposes of SOP 94-3 have been met. However, these factors *do* give a general idea of the things that the organizations should be considering when determining whether control exists.

Tip   Consider the following set of circumstances to get an idea of the complexity of some of the relationships between and among not-for-profit organizations: The residents of Avenue A set up a not-for-profit civic organization to promote the well-being of their street, which includes planting trees, sponsoring block parties, and so on. The residents of Avenues B and C think this is a great idea and set up their own not-for-profit civic associations. The residents of the whole neighborhood decide that there are broad neighborhood-wide issues and set up an additional not-for-profit neighborhood development organization to cover the ABC neighborhood. The businesses in the area see the positive result of the neighborhood development organization and set up yet another not-for-profit organization that is a business improvement district. The difficulty of determining whether any or all of these organizations are affiliates of another is compounded by the extent that all of the organizations share revenues, fund each other's activities, have common board members, share staff and office expenses, and so on. It is a very complicated area, and it is likely that many organizations that are affiliated under the accounting rules are not conforming with the accounting rules for affiliated organizations.

Economic Interest

Economic interest is defined by SOP 94-3 to exist if "(1) the other entity holds or utilizes significant resources that must be used for the unrestricted or restricted purposes of the not-for-profit organization, either directly or indirectly, by producing income or providing services, or (2) the reporting organization is responsible for the liabilities of the other entity."

SOP 94-3 offers these examples of economic interests:

Other entities solicit funds in the name of and with the expressed or implied approval of the reporting organization, and substantially all of the funds solicited are intended by the contributor or are otherwise required to be transferred to the reporting organization or used at its discretion or direction.

A reporting organization transfers significant resources to another entity whose resources are held for the benefit of the reporting organization.

A reporting organization assigns significant functions to another entity.

A reporting organization provides or is committed to provide funds for another entity or guarantees significant debt of another entity.

Using the explanations of ownership, control, and economic interest as prescribed by SOP 94-3, the following guidance should be used to determine when the financial statements of one not-for-profit organization should be consolidated with those of another not-for-profit organization. Consider the different results for each of the following scenarios:

Scenario 1   *Ownership of a majority voting interest.* A not-for-profit organization should consolidate another not-for-profit organization in which it has a controlling financial interest through direct or indirect ownership of a majority voting interest, unless control is likely to be temporary or if control does not rest with the majority owner, in which case the organizations should not be consolidated.

Scenario 2   *Control and economic interest.* A not-for-profit organization should consolidate another not-for-profit organization if the reporting not-for-profit organization has both control of the other not-for-profit organization, as evidenced by either majority ownership or a majority voting interest in the board of the other not-for-profit organization, and an economic interest in the other not-for-profit organization. If control is likely to be temporary or does not rest with the majority owner, the organizations should not be consolidated.

Scenario 3   *Economic interest but no control by majority ownership or majority voting interest.* A not-for-profit organization may exercise control of another not-for-profit organization in which it has an economic interest by means other than majority ownership or a majority voting interest in the board of the other not-for-profit organization. The factors discussed under the definition of control (other than control through voting interest) should be considered. In such circumstances, the not-for-profit organization is permitted, but not required, to consolidate the other organization. If the consolidation option is not selected in this case, there are certain disclosures about the other organization that are required in the notes to the financial statements. If control is likely to be temporary, the organizations should not be consolidated.

Scenario 4   *Either control or economic interest.* If either (but not both) control or an economic interest exists, the notes to the financial statement should contain disclosures about the other not-for-profit organization as if it were a related party. These disclosure requirements are discussed later in this chapter.

If the preceding discussion sounds confusing, that is because it *is* confusing. Here is a quick recap: In both Scenarios 1 and 2, consolidation of the other not-for-profit organization into the financial statements of the reporting not-for-profit organization is required. (As in all of the scenarios, if control is only temporary, then consolidation is not appropriate and, in fact, is not permitted.) In Scenario 3, consolidation is optional. If consolidation is not chosen, then certain disclosures must be made in the notes to the financial statements of the reporting not-for-profit organization. In Scenario 4, consolidation is not permitted, but certain disclosures about related parties need to be considered for inclusion in the notes to the financial statements.

Determining whether another organization is consolidated into the financial statements of a reporting not-for-profit organization is a decision that should not be taken lightly. The decision should be made by the management of the not-for-profit organization (since it is responsible for the fair presentation of the financial statement in accordance with GAAP) with the consultation of the organization's accounting management. It is also very important for the not-for-profit organization to consult with its independent auditors for two reasons. First, the independent auditors will need to agree with the decision as to whether the affiliated not-for-profit organization is consolidated into the financial statements of the reporting not-for-profit organization. Second, if the independent auditors will be reporting on the consolidated financial statements of the reporting organization, they will need to make sure that the financial information of the affiliated organization (most likely this will be in the form of the individual financial statements of the affiliated organization) is audited either by themselves or by another independent auditor on whose report they will rely in order to give an opinion on the consolidated financial statements.

Consolidated Financial Statements

The above discussion centers around whether the financial statements of an affiliated organization are consolidated into the financial statements of a reporting not-for-profit organization. This discussion assumes that the reader knows what consolidated financial statements are, which may not be the case. While the mechanics of preparing consolidated financial statements are more appropriate for an advanced accounting course, rather than an accounting guide for non-accountants, the basic principles are easy to understand and are described below.

The best way to think of consolidated financial statements is to first think of the separate financial statements (statement of financial position, statement of activities, and statement of cash flows) of the reporting not-for-profit organization (into which the affiliated organization will be consolidated) and the separate financial statements of the affiliated organization. The basic principle of consolidation is to add the two separate financial statements together by adding the separate statements' line items together. For example, the reporting organization's cash line is added to the affiliated organization's cash line, receivables to receivables, revenues to revenues, expenses to expenses, and so on.

If you are thinking, "What's so hard about this?" you are right. Be aware, however, that complications arise when there are transactions between the reporting and the affiliated organizations. Generally speaking, in preparing consolidated financial statements, any transactions and balances between the two organizations are eliminated. For example, if the affiliated organization owes the reporting organization $10,000, the affiliated organization's financial statements reflect a payable (liability) of $10,000, and the reporting organization's financial statements reflect a receivable (asset) of $10,000. Viewing the two organizations as one consolidated financial reporting entity, however, the reporting entity cannot owe itself money. Accordingly, in the consolidated financial statements, neither the payable nor the receivable is reflected on the statement of financial position. They are both eliminated as part of the consolidation process.

A similar concept applies to the statement of activities where transactions between the two entities are eliminated. For example, if the affiliate makes a contribution to the reporting organization, the affiliate records a contribution expense and the reporting organization records contribution revenue. Both of these amounts would be eliminated as part of the process of preparing consolidated financial statements. (Note that if the affiliate receives contributions from donors that it ultimately passes to the reporting organization, the consolidated financial statements will still reflect these amounts as contribution revenues because they are transactions between the affiliated organization and third parties, which are not eliminated.) It is the transfer of these assets to the reporting organization that is eliminated. This prevents the contribution revenue from being "doubled-up," in that it is not reported by both the affiliate and the reporting organization in the consolidated financial statements. Note that, after consideration of the requirements relative to pass-through grants discussed in Chapter 3, the separate financial statements of the affiliated organization may reflect the contribution revenue without elimination.

Another factor to consider in consolidating an affiliated not-for-profit organization is to make sure that the nature of the assets and liabilities that are being combined do not lose their distinctions in consolidations. For example, the temporarily or permanently restricted assets of an affiliated organization should be reported as part of the temporarily or permanently restricted net assets of the consolidated organization. Similarly, if the affiliated organization has restricted cash on its statement of financial position, this amount should not be added to the reporting entity's unrestricted cash and reported on one cash line. If the affiliate required a separate line for restricted cash, this line should carry through to the consolidated financial statements (or be added to the reporting organization's restricted cash, if it has this line item in its own financial statements).

An additional complication of consolidation occurs when there are other owners of the affiliated organization. Remember that in the scenario involving ownership of shares, only majority ownership is required, not full ownership. Consolidation principles require that recognition be given in the financial statements (through the recording of an account called *minority interest*, which is like a liability account) to the fact that the reporting organization may not "own" all of the affiliated organization that is being consolidated.

Caution   The other factor that complicates consolidation is the adjustments that may be required in the year that the reporting entity obtains ownership, control, and so on, of the affiliated organization. The above discussion focuses on consolidation on an ongoing basis, but what happens when an event (similar to a purchase in the commercial environment) occurs that results in a previously unaffiliated organization now requiring consolidation? Should the newly affiliated organization's assets and liabilities be recorded at their book value or should they be recorded at their fair value on the date of the purchase-like event? This topic is covered in Chapter 12, which deals with accounting developments, as this is a topic currently under consideration by the FASB.

FOR-PROFIT SUBSIDIARIES

Not-for-profit organizations sometimes make investments in for-profit entities. In some cases, these investments are made to account for investments where the objective is a maximization of profits. For example, a not-for-profit organization that desires to invest in real estate may form a wholly owned, for-profit corporation that purchases and manages an office building. On the other hand, a not-for-profit organization may set up a for-profit subsidiary for tax considerations. For example, if a not-for-profit organization expects to generate a significant amount of unrelated business income through the sale of merchandise bearing its insignia or trademark (such as clothing, coffee mugs, etc.), there may be tax advantages to having these activities managed and accounted for through a for-profit subsidiary.

SOP 94-3 provides these guidelines to not-for-profit organizations accounting for investments in for-profit entities:

1. A reporting not-for-profit organization should consolidate a for-profit entity in which it has a controlling financial interest through direct or indirect ownership of a majority voting interest if GAAP for commercial enterprises requires consolidation. The manner in which the for-profit entity's financial position, results of operations, and cash flows are presented in the reporting organization's financial statement depends on the nature of the activities of the for-profit entity. Again, the topic of recent developments in business combinations involving not-for-profit organizations is discussed in Chapter 12.

2. A reporting not-for-profit organization should use the equity method to report investments in common stock of a for-profit entity if GAAP requires the use of the equity method.

The consolidation principles that would apply to consolidating a for-profit entity with a reporting not-for-profit organization are similar to those described above for consolidating two not-for-profit organizations. An overview of the equity method of accounting for an investment in a for-profit entity is described in Chapter 4.

The general rules for determining whether to use the equity method or consolidation is generally based on the percentage of ownership of the voting shares of the for-profit subsidiary. If the not-for-profit organization owns more than 50% of the voting shares of the for-profit subsidiary, there is a presumption that consolidation is appropriate. If the not-for-profit organization owns from 20% to 50% of the voting shares of the for-profit subsidiary, there is a presumption that the equity method should be used. If less than 20% of the voting shares of the for-profit company are owned, there is a presumption that the investment in the for-profit company should be treated as any other equity investment, as described in Chapter 4.

The use of the word *presumption* above is deliberate. Since the actual selection of method to use comes down to control, there may be instances where, because of specific circumstances, for example, a less than 50% voting interest might still give a not-for-profit organization control, consolidation might be appropriate. At the same time, if control is likely to be temporary, then GAAP prohibits consolidation, even if the not-for-profit organization currently owns more than 50% of the voting shares of the for-profit company. Similarly, a not-for-profit organization that owns 30% of a for-profit subsidiary may have so little influence or control over the for-profit company that the equity method may not be appropriate, even though the ownership interest exceeds 20%.

RELATED PARTY DISCLOSURES

Not-for-profit organizations, particularly smaller organizations, are notorious for having many related party transactions. Just because a transaction is deemed a related party transaction does not mean that there is something wrong with the transaction. It simply means that, because of the requirements of FASB Statement No. 57, "Related Party Disclosures" (SFAS 57), certain disclosures may have to be made about the transaction, if it is material.

Who (or What) Are Related Parties?

SFAS 57 defines a related party as an entity that can control or significantly influence the management or operating policies of another entity to the extent one of the entities may be prevented from pursuing its own interests. A related party may be any party the entity deals with that can exercise that control. Examples of related parties include (1) affiliates, (2) investments accounted for under the equity method, (3) trusts for the benefit of employees (for example, pension or profit-sharing trusts), and (4) members of management, the governing board, and their immediate families.

The fact that members of management and the government board (and their immediate families) are considered related parties to a not-for-profit organization may come as a surprise to someone not previously familiar with related party disclosure requirements. That is why simple transactions, such as a board member leasing office space to a not-for-profit organization, need to be disclosed in the notes to the not-for-profit organization's financial statements, assuming the transactions are not insignificant. What may also be surprising is that the transaction would be disclosed regardless of whether the office space was being provided for free, at a discounted rate, at a fair value for similar office space, or at a higher than fair value rate.

Other individuals or entities that may be considered related parties of not-for-profit organizations include:

- Significant contributors (but only if they can significantly influence management or operating policies of the organization to an extent that the organization is prevented from pursuing its own interests)

- Entities whose officers or directors are also members of another organization's governing board
- Separate entities that solicit funds in the name of the organization and substantially all of the funds solicited are intended for the use of the organization
- An affiliate that is either controlled by a parent organization or where an economic interest exists (but not both)

SFAS 57 provides that transactions between related parties should be recorded in the same manner as transactions between unrelated parties. That is, their substance, rather than their form, should generally govern the accounting. Here are examples of common related party transactions:

- Sales, purchases, and transfers of property
- Services received or furnished
- Property and equipment leases
- Borrowing or lending, including guarantees
- Maintenance of compensating bank balances for the benefit of a related party
- Filing annual group information and tax returns (for organizations that have established their tax-exempt status under a group exemption letter)

Here are examples of related party transactions that are common to not-for-profit organizations, particularly smaller organizations:

- Purchases of goods or services from board members
- Payment to, or receipts from, affiliated organizations
- Office space leased from, or donated by, board members or related entities
- Personal assets guaranteed or pledged by the organization's board members

Not considered related party transactions under the rules of SFAS 57, however, are compensation arrangements and expense reimbursements. For example, the executive director is considered a related party, but paying the executive director a salary would not be considered a related party transaction. In addition, if the not-for-profit organization reimburses a board member for travel expenses incurred in attending the organization's board meeting, this reimbursement would not be considered a related party transaction.

The requirements of SFAS 57 are disclosure oriented, not accounting oriented. The following summarizes the disclosure requirements for material related party transactions:

- The nature of the relationship
- A description of the transaction
- The dollar amount of the transaction(s) during the fiscal year
- Amounts due to and from related parties at the fiscal year-end

Note that if related party amounts are eliminated when consolidated financial statements are prepared (such as the transactions and balances between a reporting not-for-profit organization and its consolidated affiliated organization), the related party disclosures listed above would *not* be required for the transactions or balances that were eliminated. This makes sense, since the transactions and balances that have been eliminated are no longer reflected in the financial statements. If the organizations issue stand-alone financial statements and have related party transactions that are not eliminated, the disclosures requirements of SFAS 57 would apply to the stand-alone financial statements of the individual not-for-profit organizations.

SUMMARY

This chapter described the accounting for not-for-profit organizations that are affiliated. It described how a reporting organization determines whether it should or should not consolidate the finan-

cial statements of an affiliated organization into its own consolidated financial statements. Also discussed were the accounting
implications when a not-for-profit organization owns or invests in
a for-profit entity. Finally, an overview of the required disclosures
for related party transactions was presented. In practice, many not-
for-profit organizations are interrelated in a number of different
ways with other not-for-profit organizations. Learning how to sort
out the different accounting applied to different relationships is
an important step in understanding the financial statements of not-
for-profit organizations.

CHAPTER 7

Collections

This chapter describes how not-for-profit organizations account for collections. The collections covered in this chapter are the historical or artistic treasures found in museums and art galleries—*not* those in which a collection canister (or hat) is passed around and the not-for-profit organization accounts for the nickels, dimes, and quarters that are collected.

The accounting rules for collections were set by the FASB in Statement No. 116, "Accounting for Contributions Received and Contributions Made" (SFAS 116). At the time SFAS 116 was issued, the accounting for collections was a very contentious issue for not-for-profit organizations. The problems centered around valuing the recording of collections that had been donated to not-for-profit organizations. Arguably, determining the fair value of a collection of historical artifacts that is donated in the current year to a museum is a difficult, though not impossible, task. The bigger challenge would have been to value all of the collections currently owned by not-for-profit organizations. This would have created a costly accounting requirement for not-for-profit organizations to meet, while at the same time resulting in information that many considered to be of limited value.

These controversies resulted in a set of accounting rules for collections that are, shall we say, flexible. While the answer to the question "How should a not-for-profit organization account for its collections?" is not exactly *"Any way it wants to,"* the answer is not far off from that.

WHAT IS A COLLECTION?

SFAS 116 provides a specific definition of what it considers to be collections. Collections are works of art, historical treasures, and similar assets that are:

- Held for public exhibition, education, or research in furtherance of public service rather than financial gain.
- Protected, kept unencumbered, cared for, and preserved.
- Subject to an organizational policy that requires that the proceeds from the sales of collection items be used to acquire other items for collections.

These guidelines can usually be applied to particular circumstances in determining whether certain items constitute a collection without too much difficulty. Art, historical, and other types of museums will generally have exhibitions of items that will meet the definition of a collection.

To illustrate an example of what a collection is, consider the difference between an art museum and an art gallery. Both are likely to have lots of paintings hanging on the walls that people walk around and look at. However, the purposes of the museum and the gallery are different. The museum preserves its art pieces, yet displays them for public viewing. While it may charge an admission fee, the purpose of the fee is usually to recover costs rather than to "cash in" on its valuable asset. Art items are not for sale, although the museum may elect to sell or exchange certain pieces, provided that the proceeds (or the artwork received in exchange) are used to replace the item in the collection. The art gallery (which may not be a not-for-profit organization to begin with) is specifically in the business of selling art. Its job is to sell the art, not preserve it. There are no limitations on the sales proceeds that it receives from purchasers of the artwork that it sells (other than returning the agreed-on amount to the artist who created the artwork).

ACCOUNTING FOR COLLECTIONS

A not-for-profit organization has three options in determining its accounting for collections. The most important thing to remember, however, is that once an accounting policy is established for collections, it must be applied by the not-for-profit organization consistently. The not-for-profit organization cannot pick and choose the accounting for its various collections. The policy must be consistently applied, both currently and in the future. Each option focuses on whether or not the cost or value of the collection is capitalized. *Capitalized* means that the cost or value is recorded as an asset on the statement of financial position. The three options are:

- Capitalize all collections
- Capitalize only collection items acquired after the adoption of SFAS 116
- Do not capitalize any collection items

The following paragraphs describe the accounting for each of these three options.

All Collection Items Are Capitalized

Collection items that are acquired in exchange transactions (that is, purchased) should be recognized as assets in the period acquired and should be measured at cost. This treatment is consistent with any other type of capital asset purchase.

Donated collection items should be recognized at their fair value in the period received. These items should be recorded as assets and as contribution revenue. Fair value, in concept, is generally based on quoted market prices. However, many collection items are unique and are unlikely to have quoted market prices. This uniqueness is what makes them collection items in the first place. If market prices are not available, fair value may be based on quoted market prices of similar items, appraisals, or other valuation techniques. For collections, appraisals are a likely source of information. Remember, the donor is also likely to be interested in determining fair value for tax consideration, so it is usual for an estimate of fair value to be made on behalf of the donor for items added to collections as a result of a donation.

Major uncertainties about the future service potential or economic benefit of contributed collection items may indicate that they should not be recognized. In other words, not-for-profit organizations should be careful about not recording as assets collection-type items that are not of the quality or quantity to make them practical for the not-for-profit organization to exhibit.

In cases where the collection items were not capitalized prior to the adoption of SFAS 116, the not-for-profit organization may find it difficult, if not impossible, to obtain the original cost or fair value of the collection at the time of contribution. If this is the case, the organization may value the collection:

- At the cost or fair values of the items at the time they were acquired, or
- At the cost or current market values of the items at the date SFAS 116 was adopted, whichever is more practical.

Since we are well past the required implementation date of SFAS 116, all of these considerations should have already been addressed by a not-for-profit organization's election as to whether it will capitalize its collections.

Collection Items Not Capitalized

Some organizations elect a policy of not capitalizing collections, which is acceptable under SFAS 116, assuming the item involved meets the definition of a collection item described earlier. In these cases, collection items should not be recognized either as an asset or as contribution revenue. This accounting treatment is allowable even if an item is purchased rather than received by a donor.

The following describes how the organization should report information in the financial statements in cases where the collection items are not capitalized. The statement of activities should report:

- Costs of collection items purchased as a decrease in the appropriate class of net assets. In other words, these costs are treated as an expense, rather than as an asset.
- Proceeds from the sale of collection items as an increase in the appropriate class of net assets. Since there is no asset recorded, the entire proceeds represent a gain as a result of the sale.
- Proceeds from insurance recoveries of lost or destroyed collection items as an increase in the appropriate class of net assets. Again, since there is no asset recorded, the entire proceeds represent a gain on the recovery from lost or damaged items.

Collections should be shown on the face of the statement, separately from revenues, expenses, gains, and losses. The statement of financial position should present a separate line item which has no dollar amounts for the collection items. Cash flows from purchases, sales, and insurance recoveries of items that have not been capitalized should be reported as investing activities on the statement of cash flows.

If an organization donates a noncapitalized collection item to another not-for-profit entity, the contribution made should not be shown on the face of the financial statements but should be disclosed in the notes.

Collections Capitalized After SFAS 116 Was Adopted

If the not-for-profit organization's policy is to only capitalize collection items after the adoption of SFAS 116, then accounting would be the same as for capitalized collections as described above.

In some cases, works of art that do not meet the definition of a collection require special consideration. These items should be recorded as assets at cost if purchased through an exchange transaction, or at fair value if received as a contribution. Works of art should be presented separately on the statement of financial position and recognized in a statement of activities as support that increases the appropriate net asset classes. Alternatively, these items may be disclosed in the notes to the financial statements.

SUMMARY

The accounting for collections affects only a limited number of not-for-profit organizations. Understanding the accounting requirements and the flexibility permitted in accounting policies for items that are part of collections that meet the definition of SFAS 116 is very important for these not-for-profit organizations. When a not-for-profit organization has collections, these collections may represent a very large portion of their assets, if recorded. Consistency in the application of the adopted accounting policy relative to collections is key in order to comply with GAAP in this area.

CHAPTER 8

Split-Interest Agreements

Not-for-profit organizations sometimes enter into agreements with donors for contributions in which both the donor and the not-for-profit organization retain a legal and economic interest. The interest is "split" between the donor and the not-for-profit organization, resulting in these agreements often being referred to as split-interest agreements. Variations of the types and formats of split-interest agreements are limited only by the imaginations of fund-raising executives and donors, of course within the bounds of the applicable income, estate, and gift tax laws.

The accounting and financial reporting for split-interest agreements is difficult to explain for two basic reasons. First, the not-for-profit organization has to handle the recognition of its interest in the agreement as the contribution of an asset by a donor, while at the same time giving accounting recognition to the not-for-profit organization's obligation to provide the donor with its interest in the donated asset. Second, the term split-interest agreement is a generic term that is applied to many different types of agreements entered into by donors and not-for-profit organizations. This chapter describes some of the common types of split-interest agreements that are detailed in the AICPA's *Audit and Accounting Guide for Not-for-Profit Organizations*. However, there may be any number of nuances or deviations from these basic agreements that need to be considered when determining the proper accounting treatment for these types of agreements.

ACCOUNTING FUNDAMENTALS

In understanding the basic accounting for requirements for split-interest agreements, a basic understanding of a simplistic type of agreement is helpful. Let us assume that a donor would like to make a significant contribution of assets to the donor's alma mater in the form of a portfolio of stocks and bonds (equities and debt instruments, to use the correct accounting terminology). However, the donor, now retired, needs the income from this investment portfolio to meet his or her day-to-day living expenses. The donor might enter into an agreement in which the donor transfers the interest in the investment portfolio to the not-for-profit organization, but still retains the right to all (or some fixed amount or percentage) of the investment income generated by the investment portfolio during the remainder of the donor's life. When the donor dies, the not-for-profit organization gets the full interest in the investment portfolio, meaning that the investment portfolio would become free of any donor restrictions (or remain permanently restricted, if that is what is specified by the donor) and the not-for-profit organization would have the use of the future investment income generated by the investment portfolio (or the donor may restrict the use of the investment income by the not-for-profit organization, if the donor so desires).

In the typical split-interest agreement, a donor makes a contribution either to a trust or directly to the not-for-profit organization. The not-for-profit organization has a beneficial interest in the contribution, but is not the sole beneficiary. Some split-interest agreements do not permit donors to legally revoke their gift. These are called irrevocable split-interest agreements. Other types of split-interest agreements may permit the donor to revoke the agreement (and the contribution) in certain situations. These are called revocable split-interest agreements. The time period covered by the split-interest agreement is expressed either as a specific number of years or as the remaining life of an individual or individuals designated by the donor.

The assets may be invested and administered by the not-for-profit organization, a trustee, or a fiscal agent. Distributions may be made to a single beneficiary or to multiple beneficiaries during the term of the agreement. At the end of the agreement's term, the remaining assets covered by the agreement are distributed to or retained by either the not-for-profit organization or another beneficiary or beneficiaries.

There are two basic types of split-interest agreements: revocable and irrevocable. A not-for-profit organization should determine whether the agreement is revocable or irrevocable when it is notified of, or receives assets under, a split-interest agreement.

REVOCABLE SPLIT-INTEREST AGREEMENTS

A revocable split-interest agreement should be accounted for as an intention to give, meaning that contribution revenue is *not* recorded when the agreement is executed. Assets received by not-for-profit organizations acting as a trustee under revocable split-interest agreements should be recognized at fair value when received and as a liability, usually called refundable advances. In other words, they are not recognized as contribution revenue, even for the not-for-profit's beneficial interest, because the donor has the option to revoke the agreement. The transferred assets are reported on the statement of financial position as assets, with a corresponding liability to return them to the donor.

Changes in the carrying value of assets received under revocable split-interest agreements and income from those assets that is not available for the organization's unconditional use should be recognized as adjustments to the recorded assets and related refundable advance liability. However, if income generated by assets is available for the organization's unconditional use, it should be recognized as either unrestricted, temporarily restricted, or permanently restricted contribution revenue, depending on the existence or absence of donor restrictions. In other words, in this case, the not-for-profit has no obligation to return the income to the donor, so it would recognize this income as contribution revenue.

Assets received under a revocable split-interest agreement

should be recognized as contribution revenue only when the agreement becomes irrevocable or the assets become available to the organization for its unconditional use, whichever occurs first.

IRREVOCABLE SPLIT-INTEREST AGREEMENTS

An irrevocable split-interest agreement is one that cannot be canceled by the donor. In the absence of donor-imposed conditions, not-for-profit organizations should recognize contribution revenue and related assets and liabilities when irrevocable split-interest agreements naming them trustee or fiscal agent are executed. In other words, the not-for-profit organization recognizes its share of its interest in the agreement, while at the same time recognizes that it has a liability to one or more other beneficiaries.

On the date of initial recognition of a split-interest agreement, contributions should be measured at fair value. The fair value of the contribution may be estimated directly, based on the present value of the estimated future distributions expected to be received by the not-for-profit organization as a beneficiary. This technique is used when a not-for-profit organization's interest in the agreement is a series of payments received over a period of time.

In some cases, future distributions will be received by the not-for-profit organization only after obligations to other beneficiaries are satisfied. In these cases, the fair value of the contribution may be estimated based on the fair value of the assets contributed by the donor less the present value of the payments expected to be made to other beneficiaries.

Methods for measuring the fair value of the contribution would normally consider a series of factors including:

- The estimated return on the invested assets during the expected term of the agreement
- The contractual payment obligations under the agreement
- An interest rate, called a discount rate, commensurate with the risks involved

In order to satisfy tax, accounting, and legal requirements, the assistance of an attorney or individual with similar skills may be needed, depending on the size of the contribution and the complexity of the agreement.

Contribution revenues recognized under split-interest agreements should be classified as increases in temporarily restricted net assets unless the donor has permanently restricted the not- or-profit organization's use of its interest in the assets or the donor gives the organization the immediate right to use without restrictions the assets it receives.

Under many charitable gift annuity agreements, the assets received from the donor are held by the not-for-profit organization as part of its general assets and are available for its unrestricted use. If the organization has the immediate right to use its interest without restrictions by the donor, the contribution should be classified as an increase in unrestricted net assets.

The contribution should be recorded as an increase in permanently restricted assets if the donor has permanently restricted the organization's use of its interest.

When a not-for-profit organization serves as trustee or when the assets contributed by the donor are otherwise under the control of the not-for-profit organization, cash and other assets received under split-interest agreements should be recognized at fair value at the date of initial recognition.

If those assets, or a portion of those assets, are being held for the benefit of others, a liability, measured at the present value of the expected future payments to be made to other beneficiaries, should also be recognized at the date of initial recognition. Present value calculations reflect the fact that a dollar paid in the future is not worth as much as a dollar received today. Given inflation, a dollar paid in the future has less value or purchasing power than if that dollar was paid today.

The determination of the liability that is recorded may be based on the lives of one or more beneficiaries. Accordingly, the services of an actuary may be required to determine the amount of the liability to be recorded. In some cases, the future payments can be based on the terms of the agreement. In other cases, the future payments will be made by the not-for-profit organization only after the organization receives its benefits. In those situations, the present value of the future payments to be made to other beneficiaries may be estimated by the fair value of the assets contributed by the donor under the agreement less the present value of the estimated benefits to be received by the not-for-profit organization.

In arrangements in which cash or other assets contributed by donors under split-interest agreements are held by independent trustees or by other fiscal agents of the donors, or are otherwise not controlled by the not-for-profit organization, the not-for-profit organization should recognize its beneficial interest in these assets. Contribution revenue and a receivable should be measured at the present value of the estimated future distributions expected to be received by the organization over the expected term of the agreement. In other words, the not-for-profit would not receive the donor's interest as an asset and liability since it is not holding that asset and, accordingly, does not have an obligation to pay it to the donor.

In some cases, the organization obtains new information about the split-interest agreement that will have an impact on the accounting for the transaction. For example, the donor's life expectancy may change. The changes will be classified as temporarily restricted, permanently restricted, or unrestricted net assets. This is dependent on the original classification used when the contribution was initially recorded.

When the organization is the trustee or fiscal agent for the agreement, income earned on the controlled assets, gains and losses, and distributions made to the other beneficiaries under the agreements should be reflected in the organization's statement of financial position, activities, and cash flows.

Amounts should be reclassified from temporarily restricted net assets to unrestricted net assets as distributions are received by not-for-profit organizations under the terms of split-interest agreements, unless those assets are otherwise temporarily restricted by the donor. In that case, they should be reclassified to unrestricted net assets when the restrictions expire.

Upon termination of a split-interest agreement, asset and liability accounts related to the agreement should be closed, that is, reduced to zero. Any remaining differences in amounts in the asset or liability accounts should be recognized as changes in the value of split-interest agreements and classified as changes in permanently restricted, temporarily restricted, or unrestricted net assets, as appropriate. If assets previously distributed to the not-for-profit organization become available for its unrestricted use on termination of the agreement, appropriate amounts should be reclassified from temporarily restricted to unrestricted net assets.

Financial Statement Presentation

Assets and liabilities recognized under split-interest agreements should be disclosed separately from other assets and liabilities in the statement of financial position or detailed in the related notes to the financial statements. Contribution revenue and changes in the value of split-interest agreements recognized under such agreements should also be disclosed as separate line items in the statement of activities or in the related notes.

EXAMPLES OF SPLIT-INTEREST AGREEMENTS

Here are several common types of split-interest agreements:

- Charitable lead trusts
- Perpetual trusts held by third parties
- Charitable remainder trusts
- Charitable gift annuities
- Pooled (life) income funds

A brief description of each of these types of agreements is provided to familarize the reader with several of the various types of agreements.

Charitable Lead Trust

Under a charitable lead trust, a donor establishes a trust naming a not-for-profit organization as a beneficiary. The organization's use of the assets may be restricted by the donor. Charitable lead trusts may take one of these forms:

- *Charitable lead annuity trust.* Under this type of charitable lead trust, the not-for-profit organization periodically receives a specific dollar amount from the trust.
- *Charitable lead unitrusts.* Under this type of charitable lead trust, the not-for-profit organization periodically receives a distribution of a fixed percentage of the trust's fair market value determined each year.

The accounting requirements for recording a charitable lead trust agreement depend on whether the not-for-profit organization is the trustee or otherwise controls the assets.

When the assets are held by a third-party trustee, an organization should initially record a contribution receivable and contribution revenue for the present value of the future benefits expected to be received from the trust. During the term of the agreement, the organization should record distributions as reductions of the contribution receivable account, rather than as contribution revenue.

The organization should also amortize the discount on the present value of expected benefits by increasing its contribution receivable balance and recognizing the change in value of split-interest agreements on its statement of activities (an increase or decrease in net assets). This reflects the fact that as time progresses closer to the payment receipt date, the value of the receivable increases. When a payment is actually received by the not-for-profit organization, the receivable for that payment should be equal to the amount of the payment.

If the estimated value of future benefits changes at some point during the term of the agreement, the organization should adjust its contribution receivable balance to reflect the change in value of split-interest agreements accounts as appropriate. When the trust terminates, the organization should adjust its remaining contribution receivable balance to zero and record a corresponding debit to the change in value of split-interest agreements accounts.

Perpetual Trust Held by a Third Party

A perpetual trust held by a third party is an arrangement in which a donor establishes and funds a perpetual trust administered by an individual or organization other than the not-for-profit beneficiary. Under the terms of the trust, the not-for-profit organization has the irrevocable right to receive the income earned on the trust assets in perpetuity, but never receives the assets held in trust. Distributions received by the organization may be restricted by the donor.

For example, a donor establishes a trust with the donor's bank serving as trustee. Funds contributed to the trust are to be invested in perpetuity. Under the terms of the trust, the not-for-profit organization is to be the sole beneficiary and is to receive annually the income on the trust's assets as earned in perpetuity. The not-for-profit can use the funds in any way that is consistent with its mission.

The arrangement should be recognized by the not-for-profit organization as contribution revenue and as an asset when the not-for-profit organization is notified of the trust's existence. The fair value of the contribution should be measured at the present value of the estimated future cash receipts from the trust's assets. The contribution should be classified as permanently restricted support, because the trust is similar to donor-restricted permanent endowment that the organization does not control, rather than a multiyear promise to give. Annual distributions from the trust are reported as investment income that increases unrestricted net assets. Adjustments to the amount reported as an asset, based on an annual review using the same basis as was used to measure the asset initially, should be recognized as permanently restricted gains or losses.

Charitable Remainder Trust

A donor establishes and funds a trust with specified distributions to be made to a designated beneficiary over the trust's term. Upon termination of the trust's term, the organization will receive any assets remaining in the trust and, depending on the donor's wishes, will have unrestricted or restricted use of them.

Charitable remainder trusts generally take one of these two forms:

- *Charitable remainder annuity trusts (CRAT).* Under this type of charitable remainder trust, distributions to the beneficiary are for a specified dollar amount.
- *Charitable remainder unitrusts (CRUT).* Under this type of charitable remainder trust, the beneficiary receives a stated percentage of the fair market value of the trust, determined annually. In some cases, the donor limits the CRUT distributions to the lesser of the actual amount earned or the stated distribution percentage.

Charitable Gift Annuity

Similar to a charitable remainder annuity trust, in a charitable gift annuity the donor contributes assets to a not-for-profit organization in exchange for a promise by the organization to pay a fixed amount over a specified period of time to the donor or to other third parties. It is important to note that the third parties are designated by the donor.

The agreements are similar to charitable remainder annuity trusts except that no trust exists, the assets received are held as general assets of the not-for-profit organization, and the annuity liability is a general obligation of the organization.

An example of a charitable gift annuity would be: A donor transfers assets to a not-for-profit organization in exchange for a promise by the organization to pay a specific dollar amount annually to the donor's wife until the wife dies.

An organization should record the assets received at fair value on the date of the agreement. An annuity payment liability should be recorded at the present value of the future distributions to the other third parties. Contribution revenue should be recorded for the difference between the assets received and the liability to others.

During the life of the agreement, payments made to beneficiaries should reduce the annuity liability and the cash account. In addition, the organization should amortize the present value of the expected amount to be paid to others by increasing the annuity payment liability account.

If the estimated value of future benefits to be paid to others changes (e.g., due to a change in life expectancy), the not-for-profit organization should adjust the annuity payment liability account to reflect the change. This would result in either a debit or credit to the change in the value of the split-interest agreements account.

When the agreement terminates and payments to others cease, the annuity liability account should be reduced to zero and a debit should be recorded to the split-interest agreements account.

Pooled (Life) Income Fund

Some not-for-profit organizations form, invest, and manage pooled (or life) income funds. These funds are divided into units, and contributions of many donors' life income gifts are pooled and invested as a group. Donors are assigned a specific number of units based on the proportion of the fair value of their contributions to the total fair value of the pooled income fund on the date of the donor's entry to the pooled fund. Until a donor's death, the donor is paid the actual income earned on the donor's assigned units. Upon the donor's death, the value of these assigned units reverts to the not-for-profit organization.

For example, a donor contributes assets to a not-for-profit organization's pooled income fund and is assigned a specific number of units in the pool. The donor is to receive a life interest in any income earned on those units. Upon the donor's death, the value of the units is available to the not-for-profit organization for its unrestricted use.

The not-for-profit organization should recognize its remainder interest in the assets received as temporarily restricted contribution revenue in the period in which the assets are received from the donor. The contribution should be measured at the fair value of the assets to be received, discounted for the estimated time period until the donor's death. The contributed assets should be recognized at fair value when received. The difference between the fair value of the assets when received and the revenue recognized should be recorded as deferred revenue, representing the amount of the discount for future interest.

Periodic income on the fund and payments to the donor should be reflected as increases and decreases in a liability to the donor, respectively. Amortization of the discount should be recognized as a reduction in the deferred revenue account and as a change in the value of split-interest agreements and reported as a change in temporarily restricted net assets. Upon the donor's death, any remaining balance in the deferred revenue account should be closed and a change in the value of split-interest agreements should be recognized. A reclassification to unrestricted net assets is also necessary to record the satisfaction of the time restriction on temporarily restricted net assets.

SUMMARY

The non-accountant might be frustrated trying to understand all of the requirements and circumstances involved in the accounting and financial reporting for split-interest agreements. The purpose of this chapter is not to make the reader an expert in accounting for split-interest agreements, but to familiarize the reader with, first, the existence of these types of agreements and, second, an overview of the accounting considerations that must be made. A useful suggestion is for the reader to look back at the chapter introduction, which describes the nature of split-interest agreements. Keep in mind that these are contributions in which both the not-for-profit organization and the donor retain some form of interest in the assets that are part of the agreement. The role of the accounting for split-interest agreements is to record proper values for both the irrevocable rights to assets that a not-for-profit organization receives as part of the agreement as well as any obligation that the not-for-profit organization has to the donor (or any beneficiaries specified by the donor) as a result of the agreement.

CHAPTER 9

Accounting for Pension and Other Postretirement Employee Benefit Plans

Not-for-profit organizations have gained the reputation of not paying their employees tremendous salaries, but instead providing generous benefits as part of the employees' overall compensation packages. While some of these benefits are paid for by the not-for-profit organizations currently (such as providing health-care coverage during an employee's period of active employment), other benefits are not paid until after an employee retires. Benefits paid after retirement include pension benefits and, in many cases, health insurance and similar benefits for retirees. These postretirement benefits fall into two categories:

- Pension benefits
- Other postretirement employee benefits (commonly referred to as OPEBs)

The essential focus of the accounting issues described in this chapter relate to these two types of postretirement benefits. The essential element of the accounting question relative to these two benefits is simple:

- How should the costs of providing these benefits be matched to the period of time that the services are performed by the employee?
- How should a not-for-profit organization reflect in its financial statements its obligation to provide these benefits to retirees (or former employees) in the future?

No matter how complex pension and OPEB accounting and financial reporting may seem, the basic goals of the accounting requirements, financial disclosures, actuarial calculations and methods, and so on, all come down to answering these two questions. Keeping these simple goals in mind, this chapter will delve into the accounting and financial reporting issues that relate to pension plans and OPEBs.

ACCOUNTING FOR PENSION PLANS

Pension plans are widely used as employee benefits that provide retirement benefits for many employers, including not-for-profit organizations. There are two main types of pension plans that may be offered to employees:

- Defined contribution pension plans
- Defined benefit pension plans

While not always considered a pension plan, a third type of arrangement, a deferred compensation plan, is also discussed in this chapter.

Usually an employer offers one of these types of plans, although an employer may offer both if it so desires. The accounting and financial reporting rules for defined contribution pension plans are far less complex than those for defined benefit pension plans. Both of these types of plans are discussed in the following sections of this chapter.

Defined Contribution Pension Plans

A defined contribution pension plan provides pension benefits to employees in return for the services that the employees render to the not-for-profit organization. In this type of plan, an individual account for each participant is established and the plan specifies how contributions to an individual's account are determined. When an individual employee retires, his or her pension benefit is determined based on the amount in the individual's account. The amount in an individual's account is a result of the amounts contributed to the account, the returns earned on the investments of these contributions, and, in some cases, forfeitures of other participants' benefits that have been allocated to all other participants' accounts. As can be discerned from the above, it is the amount of the contributions to the plan that is defined, and not the pension benefit itself that is defined by the plan.

The accounting for defined contribution pension plans is relatively straightforward in most cases. To the extent that the not-for-profit organization's contributions that are defined under the plan are made to the plan during the accounting periods in which the individuals render services, the pension expense recorded by the not-for-profit organization is equal to the amount of the contribution.

Practical Example   A defined benefit contribution plan specifies that 3% of an employee's salary is contributed to the plan. The contributions are made on a monthly basis. If the employee's annual salary is $60,000, his or her monthly salary is $5,000. The monthly contribution is calculated as 3% of $5,000, or $150. The not-for-profit organization records an expense of $150 in the month in which the employee earns the $5,000. If the employee's salary increases during the year, the amount of the contribution increases and the corresponding pension expense recorded by the not-for-profit organization increases by the same amount.

The above example assumes that the not-for-profit organization is only obligated to make contributions to the pension plan while the employee is providing services to the not-for-profit organization. If the employee leaves the organization for another job, in most cases, the not-for-profit organization has no obligation to keep contributing to the pension plan. If there is some provision in the pension plan, however, which causes the not-for-profit organization to be required to contribute to the plan after the employee has ceased providing services to the not-for-profit organization, the accounting becomes more complicated. The not-for-profit organization would accrue the expense for these postemployment contributions to the periods of time in which the employee is providing services. This type of arrangement is more the exception than the rule, and the mechanics of the calculations would be beyond the scope of this book, but the reader should be aware of this potential complication caused by the timing of the contributions being different from the time that services are rendered to the organization by the employee.

Contributions to pension plans, including defined contribution plans, are generally held by a trustee on behalf of the pension plan and its sponsoring employer. Accordingly, the assets of a pension plan, including those of a defined contribution pension plan, would not be recorded as assets of the not-for-profit organization employer. These are not assets of the not-for-profit organization. At the same time, assuming that the contributions required to be made by the not-for-profit organization to the defined benefit pension plan are made timely during the period of employment of the covered employee, there is no further liability to the pension plan by the not-for-profit organization. Whatever assets accumulated in an individual's account as a result of contribution and investment earnings will determine the amount of an employee's pension. In a defined benefit pension plan, there is no liability for future pension benefits that needs to be recorded by the not-for-profit organization. A liability that might be recorded by a not-for-profit organization is one to account for the difference in time between when a contribution amount is calculated and due to the defined contribution pension plan and when the cash payment is actually made to the pension plan. This should only be a short-term liability. For example, using the same facts as in the previous example, let us assume that the not-for-profit organization has a fiscal year-end of June 30. The $150 monthly contribution based on the employee's salary during the month of June may not actually be contributed to the plan until July. The $150 July payment for the month of June would be accrued to the fiscal year ending June 30, meaning that a liability would be recorded on the statement of financial position as of June 30 and an additional $150 of pension expense would be recorded.

Defined Benefit Pension Plans

A defined benefit pension plan, as its name suggests, is a pension plan that defines an amount of pension benefit that will be provided to the retiree. The defined benefit is *not* a specific dollar amount. Rather, it is an amount that is a calculation determined by what is often called the pension plan's pension benefit formula. The pension benefit formula takes into consideration a number of factors, depending on the specific provisions of the plan, that affect the amount of monthly pension benefit that a retiree will receive. These factors vary with each particular defined benefit pension plan, but usually include such factors as an employee's length of service and the employee's level of compensation. More on these factors will be discussed later in this section.

The accounting for defined benefit pension plans is more complicated than that for defined contribution pension plans. Here is why. A basic underlying principle in GAAP accounting is to match the recording of an expense with the period of time that is benefited from whatever was purchased with the expense. In the case of a defined benefit pension plan, employees earn the right to receive a pension during the time that they work for the not-for-profit organization. That right to a pension at retirement is part of the cost of the services that employees provide. Generally accepted accounting principles require that an expense for these future defined pension benefits be recorded by the not-for-profit organization during the time that the employee works for the not-for-profit organization.

DETERMINING PENSION EXPENSE

A key component in accounting for a defined benefit pension plan is determining the annual amount of pension expense that should be recorded by a not-for-profit organization. The non-accountant might justifiably ask why the amount of the not-for-profit organization's annual contribution to its defined benefit pension would not automatically be the amount of pension expense that the not-for-profit organization would recognize for that year. The answer is that it might be, but it is not necessarily the same amount. Under GAAP, the annual contribution by an employer to a defined benefit pension plan is computed by an actuary. (Keep in mind that there are a number of federal laws and regulations that govern pension plans that affect how a plan is managed and funded by an employer. These requirements are important, but are beyond the scope of this book.) GAAP provides certain requirements that must be followed by the actuary in computing the annual pension cost. If the not-for-profit organization contributes the annual pension cost to the plan, the annual contribution will equal the annual pension expense recorded in the financial statements of the not-for-profit organization. However, the amount of pension expense recorded in the financial statements is the amount of annual pension cost computed by the actuary using the guidance of GAAP as well as practices that are acceptable under actuaries' professional standards. If the not-for-profit organization contributes a different amount to the defined benefit pension plan, it is the annual pension cost calculated by the actuary that is reflected in the financial statements as pension expense, even if the not-for-profit organization does not make an actual cash contribution to the pension plan. Conversely, if the not-for-profit organization contributes more to the plan than the amount calculated by the actuary, the amount in excess of the annual pension cost calculated by the asset is recorded as an asset (prepaid pension costs) rather than as an expense. In other words, regardless of the amount actually contributed by a not-for-profit organization to a defined benefit pension plan, the annual pension expense recognized in the financial statements is based on the annual pension cost computed by the actuary.

Tip   The above discussion assumes that a not-for-profit organization sponsors its own defined benefit pension plan to provide benefits to its employees. In certain circumstances, a not-for-profit organization may participate in a multiemployer defined benefit pension plan, where the contributions of several employers (either related or unrelated) are commingled. A multiemployer plan essentially bills its participating employers for the amount of their required annual contribution. The amount billed is determined by the plan's actuary, in a similar manner as described in this section. The not-for-profit organization should recognize whatever amount it is billed by the multiemployer plan as its annual pension expense.

DETERMINING PENSION LIABILITY

A second key part of the calculations performed by the actuary is determining the liability for future pension benefits that must be provided by the plan. There are two different views of this future liability. They are termed the accumulated benefit obligation and the projected benefit obligation. Here is a brief synopsis of each. (The reader will have a better understanding of what goes into the calculation of these amounts after reading the later sections of this chapter. For now, it is important to understand the effect of the amounts that result from these calculations on the financial statements of the not-for-profit organization.)

Accumulated Benefit Obligation

This amount represents the actuarially calculated present value of all future pension benefits (as calculated by the pension benefit formula) that have been earned by employees up to the date of the calculation, based on the employees' current and past compensation levels. In other words, if we froze the world at the date of the actuarial calculation, how much money it would take to pay off all current and future retirees based on the benefits that they have earned to date. In addition, since these benefits will be paid over a period of time, this amount is calculated in current dollars (that is, their present value), which would result in an amount that is less than the actual dollars that will be paid out.

Projected Benefit Obligation

This amount represents almost the same thing as the accumulated benefit obligation, except that it recognizes that we cannot really freeze the world in time and it is likely that current employees will receive raises in the future. If the calculation of pension benefits takes into consideration salaries (which most plans do), then the projected benefit obligation takes into consideration future salary increases. Accordingly, the projected benefit obligation amount will be higher than the accumulated benefit obligation amount.

Since we are addressing the impact of defined benefit pension plans on the financial statements of not-for-profit organizations, the reader may be guessing by now that one of these liabilities is going to wind up on the statement of financial position of the not-for-profit organization. The reader would be almost correct. Let us not forget that the pension plan has assets that are available to pay the pension benefits. As the not-for-profit organization has been making contributions to the plan, these assets have been accumulating and earning investment income. Conversely, current benefit payments are also being paid out of these assets. If the accumulated benefit obligation exceeds the amount of the plan net assets, the difference is recorded as a liability on the statement of financial position of the not-for-profit organization. This difference is called the unfunded accumulated benefit obligation. If the plan assets exceed the accumulated benefit obligation, the not-for-profit organization will not record an asset on its books for the amount by which the plan net assets exceed the accumulated benefit obligation. (In terms of a pension plan, the term net assets is similar to that as it relates to not-for-profit organizations, meaning it is the amount by which the plan's assets exceed the plan's liabilities.)

Note The actuarial assumptions and calculations described in the next section are designed so that if the not-for-profit organization contributes the actuarially determined amounts over a period of time, the plan assets should at least equal the accumulated benefit obligation, resulting in no liability being recorded. Many employers were saddled with unfunded pension plans at the time of adoption of SFAS 87, and the recording of this liability was a large issue. The SFAS 87 pension cost calculation (and other federal laws and regulations mentioned previously whose impact is felt over a period of time) have diminished much of the concern over this liability, again, assuming that the actual cash contributions equal the actuarially determined pension cost. The reason for this is that contributing the annual pension cost to the defined benefit pension plan would tend to cause the plan to be fully funded, meaning that the plan net assets would equal or exceed the accumulated benefit obligation.

At the time of adoption of SFAS 87, recording the unfunded accumulated benefit obligation could have resulted in a large decrease to net assets if a not-for-profit organization had not been making its actuarially determined contributions to the pension plan over time. The FASB softened the implementation impact by allowing that an intangible asset be recorded at the time of adoption for unrecognized prior service cost. Service costs will be discussed in the following section. Suffice it to say, for the purpose of this discussion, the actuarial calculation of annual pension costs includes a component to amortize unrecognized prior service cost. This increases the amount of the actuarially calculated contribution. The intangible asset is amortized (reduced) accordingly. Since this amortization causes more assets to be put into the plan, assuming the contribution amount equals the actuarially determined annual pension cost, the unfunded accumulated benefit obligation decreases as well. (Note that any amendments to the pension plan that give additional credit for prior service by employees might also affect the amount recorded as an intangible asset.)

As we will discuss in the following sections, the calculation of the actuarially determined annual pension cost includes a component to amortize (that is, pay for) the unfunded accumulated benefit obligation. Assuming that the not-for-profit organization contributes this same amount to the plan, the theoretical result is that the increase in contributions will increase the plan's net assets and result in the ultimate elimination of the unfunded accumulated benefit obligation as a liability on the statement of financial position. Nevertheless, there are many factors that contribute to the calculation of this unfunded amount and the annual pension cost, which are discussed in the following section.

ACTUARIAL ASSUMPTIONS AND CALCULATIONS

The recording of pension expense and the calculation of the accumulated benefit obligation are clearly important for the proper accounting for defined benefit pension plans. (The calculation of the projected benefit obligation results in an amount that is an important disclosure required in the notes to the financial statements of the not-for-profit organization.) What makes the calculation of these amounts so difficult that the services of an actuary are almost always required? Using the annual pension cost as the example, consider how you would determine how much each year a particular current employee's future pension is costing the not-for-profit organization when these factors that affect the amount of that future pension are unknown at the time the employee is performing services and being paid his or her salary:

- Will the employee work at the not-for-profit organization long enough to vest in (that is, obtain a legal right to receive) his or her pension?
- How many years will the employee ultimately work for the not-for-profit organization before leaving or retiring?
- What will be the employee's salary history up to the time of his or her leaving or retiring?
- When will the employee start collecting his or her pension?
- Will the employee take advantage of plan provisions at retirement to reduce his or her benefits to cover another beneficiary, such as a spouse, with pension benefits?
- Will the employee die before retirement?
- How long will the employee (and any other beneficiaries) live after retirement? Did the type of work (clerical, manual labor, hazardous duty, etc.) affect how long he or she will be employed and how long he or she will live?
- Will there be changes in overall life expectancy in the future?
- What rate of return will the investment of the pension plan's assets produce?

Admittedly, some of these factors are quite grim, but hopefully they make the point that many, if not all, of these important questions, which, in the typical defined benefit pension plan, affect the total amount of pension benefits that will ultimately be paid out to any individual employee, are not known at the time that the employee is working and pension cost is being calculated.

GAAP specifies those factors that an actuary needs to take into consideration when calculating the annual pension cost of a defined benefit pension plan. A detailed discussion of actuarial calculations is beyond the scope of this book, but understanding some of the basics is important to understanding what expenses and liabilities are ultimately being recorded in the financial statements.

Here is an overview of some of the factors that actuaries include in calculating annual pension cost:

- *Service cost.* This is the most basic component of annual pension cost, since it represents the present value of the benefits under the pension benefit formula that have been attributed to an employee during the year. Actuaries use various cost methods to perform these calculations. These methods have names such as *projected unit credit* or *unit credit* method.
- *Interest cost.* As mentioned earlier, the projected benefit obligation represents the present value of benefits that are projected to be paid. During the course of a year, the pension plan moves one year closer to having to pay those benefits. The interest cost reflects the increase in the present value of these benefits due to the passage of time. Note that in calculating the present value, an interest discount rate must be used. This rate is selected using a number of factors, but should approximate an interest rate that reflects that average amount of time until, on average, benefits will be paid. Accordingly, employers whose employees, on the average, are very young might find it more appropriate to use a longer-term discount rate than would an employer whose employees, on the average, are very old.
- *Actual return on plan assets.* Earnings on the investment of the pension plan's assets reduce the amount that would otherwise be calculated as a pension cost of the not-for-profit organization.
- *Amortization of unrecognized prior service costs.* As mentioned above, sometimes plans are amended to give credit to employees for services rendered in the past. Since these amendments are assumed to entice employees to remain with the organization, their cost can be amortized over the estimated remaining time of employment of the employees that are covered by the amendment.
- *Gains or losses, to the extent recognized.* This is a very important concept to understand. As seen from the list of ques-

tions at the introduction of this section, actuaries make a number of assumptions about employment, longevity of employment, salary increases, inflation, rates of return on assets, mortality, and so on. They make these assumptions as part of determining service cost as well as in calculating the accumulated benefit obligation and the projected benefit obligation. As part of the actuarial calculations that are performed, actual experience, to the extent known, is compared with the assumptions and gains or losses that are calculated. These gains or losses reflect the difference between what *would have been* calculated using actual data that has become known and what *was calculated* using the various assumptions mentioned above. Actuaries know that future differences will also arise between actual data and the assumptions used and that, in many cases, these future gains and losses will offset the gains and losses that are identified as part of the current actuarial calculation.

GAAP requires the actuary to amortize these gains or losses (that is, have them affect the calculation of annual pension cost) only if they are significant. GAAP defines what is sometimes called a *corridor*, meaning that if the net of all the gains or losses falls within this defined corridor, the actuary ignores them for purposes of calculating annual pension cost. If they fall outside of the corridor, the amount by which they fall outside the corridor should be amortized as a component of annual pension cost.

- *Amortization of transition amounts.* As mentioned previously, assets or liabilities recorded with the adoption of SFAS 87 are amortized, with the annual amount of amortization being included in the calculation of annual pension cost.

REQUIRED DISCLOSURES

SFAS 87 requires a great degree of disclosures to assist the reader of the financial statements in understanding the nature of an organization's defined benefit pension plan and many of the important actuarial assumptions that go into calculating the amounts presented. The disclosures include information on the pension benefit obligation, and the value of the plan's net assets. Keep in mind that were this information not provided in the notes to the financial statements, a reader would not know this information, since it is not recorded in the financial statements. However, the funded status of the pension plan that a not-for-profit organization sponsors is an important piece of information to the reader of the not-for-profit organization's financial statements because that funded status has an impact on the future level of contributions that the not-for-profit organization will need to make to the plan.

The FASB recently reviewed the required disclosures for pension plans, including defined benefit pension plans and defined contribution pension plans. FASB Statement No. 132, "Employers' Disclosures about Pensions and Other Postretirement Benefits" (SFAS 132), fine-tunes the disclosures for these plans.

SFAS 132 contains some relief from pension plan disclosures for nonpublic organizations. Because these organizations do not have publicly traded stock or debt, they are basically not subject to the rules of the U.S. Securities and Exchange Commission. The vast majority of not-for-profit organizations will fall under this category, and can present a reduced amount of disclosures about their pension plans. While the disclosures are reduced, the key information about funding status remains a disclosure requirement. Eliminating some of the detail from these disclosures will likely improve their understandability to the reader of the notes to the financial statements.

DEFERRED COMPENSATION PLANS

Before leaving the topic of pension plans, a few words about deferred compensation plans is appropriate, since many employees of not-for-profit organizations rely heavily on these types of plans to provide for their retirement. In fact, these types of plans, for tax purposes, are actually considered the same or similar to pension plans.

As its name implies, a deferred compensation plan is a plan set up to allow an employee to elect to have a portion of his or her current earnings deferred until a future period when he or she will receive the amounts deferred along with the accumulated investment earnings. For not-for-profit organizations, these plans are commonly known as 403(b) plans, after the section of the Internal Revenue Code which governs their existence and their tax implications. These plans are similar to, but not exactly the same as, the Internal Revenue Code Section 401(k) plans offered by for-profit organizations and Section 457 plans offered by state and local governments as well as similar governmental organizations. The benefit to the employees in deferring some of their income into these plans (there are maximum amounts that can be contributed each year) is that the employee does not pay income tax on the earnings that are deferred, nor does the employee pay current income taxes on the investment earnings from the accumulated assets in the plan. The employee *does* pay tax when amounts are withdrawn from the plan. Assuming this is after retirement, the employee would then expect to be in a lower income tax bracket, providing a tax benefit. Not paying the taxes currently, but paying them in the future, creates an additional benefit to the employee.

The accounting for these types of plans is straightforward. The salary that is elected to be deferred by the employee is treated as compensation expense when earned by the employee. Instead of paying the employee (after withholding taxes), the not-for-profit organization pays the elected contribution (before withholding taxes) to the administrator of the plan. The not-for-profit organization adjusts the amount of withholding from the employee's paycheck, although this has no impact on the financial statement, other than any savings the not-for-profit organization might benefit from because of reductions in employer payroll taxes that it pays.

In some cases, the not-for-profit organization may have a policy to match, to some extent, the contributions of its employees into the deferred compensation plan. If this is the case, the not-for-profit organization would account for its required matching contributions in a manner that is consistent with the accounting of contributions to a defined contribution plan.

OTHER POSTRETIREMENT BENEFITS

Postretirement benefits include postretirement health-care benefits, life insurance provided outside of a pension plan to retirees, and other welfare benefits such as tuition assistance, day-care, legal services, and housing subsidies provided after retirement. This is not an all-inclusive list. There may be other benefits provided by not-for-profit organizations to retirees that should be considered part of OPEBs. Not-for-profit organizations are frequent providers of postretirement health-care benefits to retirees. This is probably a more popular employee benefit than providing a defined benefit pension plan for not-for-profit organizations. While the following discussion focuses on postretirement health-care benefits because they are far more popular than other types of OPEBs, the other types of benefits should not be overlooked when recording costs and liabilities in financial statements prepared in accordance with GAAP.

Historically, many organizations, including not-for-profit organizations, provided postretirement health-care benefits to employees under arrangements that were less formal than pension plans. Often these benefits were not funded at the time that the employee worked for the organization, but instead were funded on a "pay-as-you-go" basis. This means that when the health insurance was provided to the retiree and the insurance company billed the not-for-profit organization for the insurance premium, the not-for-profit paid the bill from its own assets and recognized the expense at that time for the amount billed.

As health-care costs dramatically increased over the past decade or two, it became clear that organizations, including not-for-profit organizations, were building up substantial liabilities for these obligations that were not recognized in the financial statements. As a result, the FASB issued Statement No. 106, "Employers' Accounting for Postretirement Benefits Other Than Pensions" (SFAS

106), to give recognition to these liabilities. In addition, SFAS 106 addressed the matching principle that was described above, which related to defined benefit pension plans. An employer not-for-profit organization should recognize as an expense the cost of providing OPEBs to employees during the time that the not-for-profit organization receives the benefit of the employees' work, which is the time during which they are employed.

Tip   Not-for-profit organizations may be providing postretirement benefits other than pensions to employees as a matter of historical practice and might argue that they have no legal obligation to continue to provide these benefits in the future. SFAS 106 states, however, that "Absent evidence to the contrary, it shall be presumed that an employer that has provided postretirement benefits in the past or is currently promising those benefits to employees will continue to provide those benefits." Accordingly, the lack of a specific legal requirement to provide the benefits does not relieve a not-for-profit organization of the requirements of SFAS 106. On the other hand, the prospect of adoption of SFAS 106 and the prospect of recording significant liabilities along with a considerable increase in annual expenses has caused a number of employers not only to stop providing these benefits to employees but also to explicitly state that they will not provide these benefits in the future. This provides the "evidence to the contrary" that would justify not applying SFAS 106 when these benefits have been terminated.

The good news about understanding the accounting and financial reporting for postretirement benefits other than pensions is that it works essentially the same way as the accounting and financial reporting for defined benefit pension plans. (Not everyone would agree that this is good news, but it does cut down on the number of things to learn.) Conceptually, the net periodic postretirement benefit cost is calculated with many of the same assumptions and methods as is the net periodic pension cost described above. This amount represents the postretirement benefit expense that is recognized as a reduction of net assets in the not-for-profit organization's statement of activities. Similarly, the accumulated postretirement benefit obligation can be compared conceptually to the accumulated benefit obligation for a defined benefit pension plan. The accumulated postretirement benefit obligation, offset by assets set aside to pay these benefits, is reported as a liability in the statement of financial position of the not-for-profit organization.

Since an extensive amount of information was provided about defined benefit pension plans earlier in this chapter and the accounting for OPEBs is very similar, this section will cover OPEB accounting by highlighting some of the important differences between the accounting for defined benefit pension plans and the accounting for OPEBs. In both cases, the assistance of an actuary will be required in almost all cases to perform the calculation of amounts that ultimately will be recorded in the financial statements.

Here are some of the more important differences between accounting for OPEBs and accounting for defined benefit pension plans:

- *Many OPEBs are provided without the existence of a formal plan that is a separate legal entity, as is a defined benefit pension plan.* In addition, the provision of these benefits may be in a written or unwritten agreement that contains flexibility on the part of the employer. For example, a not-for-profit organization may require its retirees to share a portion of the costs of health-care benefits that are provided. In the absence of a specific cost-sharing formula, past practice needs to be used to determine what portion of the costs are reasonably expected to be borne by the retirees in the future.
- *The sensitivity to certain assumptions about retirement age is different for postretirement benefits other than pensions.* For example, early retirement may have less of an impact on the pension calculations, while retirement prior to Medicare eligibility age may have a significant effect on the calculation of expected postretirement health-care benefits. In addi-

tion, an employee might have to be employed for a longer period of time to be eligible for a postretirement benefit other than a pension, whereas vesting in at least a partial pension benefit may begin after a much shorter time period. Accordingly, assumptions about the length of employment by employees takes on a different importance in the actuarial calculations for postretirement benefits other than pensions.

- *Assumptions about health-care coverage costs need to be made.* These would include the expected claims rate for retirees in various age categories, which will impact expected premiums. In addition, an estimate of health-care cost inflation needs to be considered, which is more difficult to estimate than a general inflation rate.

- *The propriety of offsetting assets for payment of postretirement benefits is more complicated than in defined contribution pension plans.* For assets to be offset against the recorded accumulated postretirement benefit obligation, they should be put aside in a trust specifically designated for payment of these benefits. In many cases, the investment of these assets is still within the control of the not-for-profit organization employer. Merely identifying certain assets as being set aside for payment of postretirement benefits would generally not be sufficient for offsetting them against the liability on the statement of financial position for the accumulated postretirement benefit obligation in the absence of placing these assets in a separate trust.

DISCLOSURES

Similar to pension plans, disclosures contained in the financial statements for postretirement are important to understand the assumptions and methods that were used in their calculation. SFAS 132 includes in its scope the revised disclosure requirements of postretirement benefits other than pensions. In addition, the same option to provide a reduced level of disclosure for nonpublic entities is available for postretirement benefits other than pension as is available for disclosures for defined benefit pension plans.

SUMMARY

This chapter described the interesting blend of accounting principles and actuarial methods and assumptions needed to understand a not-for-profit organization's accounting for pension benefits and other postretirement benefits other than pensions that it provides to its employees. There are two important concepts to remember. First, the accounting requirements center on matching the costs of pensions or other postretirement benefits after an employee retires with the time period that the employee actually works for the not-for-profit organization. Second, the difference in the present value of benefits accumulated under defined pension or other postretirement benefit plans and the assets of the plans from which these payments are made is recorded as a liability on the statement of financial position. Keeping these basics in mind will help in not getting lost in the details of understanding the accounting and financial reporting for these important employee benefits.

CHAPTER 10

Lease Accounting Fundamentals

Not-for-profit organizations often enter into a number of different lease agreements. Sometimes the not-for-profit organization leases something from another organization, in which case the not-for-profit organization is known as the *lessee*. Other times, the not-for-profit organization owns something and leases it to another organization. In this case the not-for-profit organization is referred to as the *lessor.*

The topic of accounting for leases means different things to different people. Some may consider leasing to involve long-lived assets, such as a not-for-profit organization entering into a long-term lease to rent office space for its administrative functions. Others may view leasing as a short-term financing mechanism— for example, the office needs new copier machines. Instead of owning and financing the copiers, they are leased for a five- or seven-year period as a substitute for obtaining financing for purchasing the copiers. Shorter term still, a not-for-profit organization may lease its automobiles under three- or four-year lease agreements. All of these are examples of leases. Lease accounting under GAAP has requirements that apply to all of these types of transactions.

The fundamental questions to be answered by lease accounting are:

- Is the substance of the transaction such that the lease is really a purchase and sale of the asset, rather than simply a rental transaction?
- Has the owner of the asset, in substance, transferred the risks and rewards of ownership to the organization that has leased and is actually using the asset?
- If it is substantively a purchase or sale of an asset, how should the transaction be reflected in the financial statements?

These fundamental questions will be addressed throughout this chapter. In addition, a secondary accounting issue concerns how to account for lease agreements that have scheduled rent increases. The answer surprises most non-accountants and is discussed in this chapter as well.

LEASE ACCOUNTING

The accounting for leases by lessors and lessees is similar, yet represents different sides of the same transaction. Since, in most cases, the not-for-profit organization will be the lessee (again, meaning that the not-for-profit organization will lease the asset from the asset's owner, which is the lessor), the focus of accounting in this chapter will be for lessees. If the reader understands the concepts behind the lessee's accounting for leases, understanding the lessor's accounting will be much easier.

OPERATING VERSUS CAPITAL LEASES

To address the accounting for leases, the most important thing is to determine whether a particular lease transaction should be classified as an operating lease or as a capital lease. This determination will drive the accounting for the lease transaction and, because the accounting for an operating lease is vastly different from that of a capital lease, this is a key determination that must be made. Most of the guidance in this determination (and the subsequent accounting treatment) is found in FASB Statement No. 13, "Accounting for Leases" (SFAS 13). Although the provisions of SFAS 13 have been fine-tuned by various later documents, its underlying fundamental principles have withstood the test of time and continue to be in use.

Determining whether a particular lease agreement is an operating or capital lease requires that the lease be tested to determine whether it is a capital lease. If a lease is not a capital lease, it is then considered to be an operating lease. There are no tests to determine whether a lease is an operating lease. Any lease that is not a capital lease is automatically an operating lease.

Tip The theory of which leases are capital leases is based on whether or not the lease agreement is, in substance, a purchase (or sale, in the case of a lessor) of an asset, with the lease being used essentially as a means to finance the purchase. Reading the criteria described below with this in mind will help these somewhat arbitrary criteria and percentages make more sense to the reader.

SFAS 13 generalizes the criteria for determination of a capital lease to mean that if substantially all of the benefits and risks of ownership have been transferred to the lessee under the lease agreement, the lease should be accounted for as a capital lease. SFAS 13 specifies that it considers substantially all of the risks or benefits of ownership to have been transferred to the lessee if any one of the following criteria have been met:

- The lease transfers ownership of the asset to the lessee by the end of the lease term.
- The lease contains a bargain purchase option.
- The lease term is equal to 75% or more of the estimated

economic life of the leased asset, and the beginning of the lease term does not fall within the last 25% of the total economic life of the leased asset.

- The present value of the minimum lease payments at the beginning of the lease term is 90% or more of the fair value of the asset in the hands of the lessor. (This criterion cannot be used if the lease's inception occurs during the last 25% of the useful economic life of the asset that is being leased.)

The first and second criteria above are fairly straightforward. If the lease states that the asset transfers to the lessee at the end of the lease, the lease is a capital lease. In substance, the lease payments are a mechanism to finance the purchase of an asset. At the same time, if a *bargain purchase option* exists, the lease is also a capital lease. In other words, if the lessee can purchase the leased property for some amount "sufficiently below" the market rate amount at the end of the lease (in some cases this is set at a nominal amount, such as $1), the lease should also be accounted for as a capital lease.

GAAP does not specifically define "sufficiently below" in this determination of whether a bargain purchase option exists, but it should be clear that there is a below-market price at the end of the lease. However, factors such as the time value of money, usage, and technological changes should be considered in determining whether there is a bargain purchase option in a lease.

Practical Example   A personal computer is leased by a not-for-profit organization for four years. At the end of the four years, the not-for-profit organization obtains the ownership of the personal computer. This would be a capital lease. Similarly, if, at the end of the four years, the not-for-profit organization had the right to purchase the personal computer for $25, it is fair to assume that this would be considered a bargain purchase and that the lease would be considered a capital lease. Even though technological advance may make the four-year-old computer significantly less valuable than when it is new, a $25 purchase option is likely to be a clear bargain, since the monitor alone would probably be worth at least a couple of hundred dollars.

The third criterion means that the lessee is leasing the property for at least 75% of its estimated life. To meet this criterion, the lease term cannot fall within the last 25% of the total economic life of the leased property.

Practical Example   A personal computer with a five-year economic life is leased by a not-for-profit organization under a four-year lease agreement. Since the lease term is four years and the economic life of the asset is five years, the lease term represents 80% of the economic life of the asset, and the lease would be considered a capital lease.

Tip   One problem in applying the third criterion is determining exactly what the term of the lease is. The lease term includes the fixed, noncancelable term of the lease increased in some cases for additional time. The additional time that may be added to the fixed noncancelable term of the lease occurs when certain factors are present in the lease, such as a bargain lease renewal clause, or if the renewal of the lease is at the discretion of the lessor. Other factors may also extend the defined term of the lease for accounting purposes, which should be considered.

The fourth criterion may be the hardest to grasp conceptually. If the total payments that will be made under the lease, adjusted for the time value of money, equal 90% or more of the fair value of the asset at the time it is leased, the transaction is, in substance, a purchase of the asset. Once again, this criterion cannot be used if the lease's inception occurs during the last 25% of the useful economic life of the asset that is being leased.

Practical Example Continuing with the personal computer example, assume that the computer has a fair value at the beginning of the lease of $2,500. Using a monthly payment of $60, the total payments under the lease are $2,880 ($60 times 12 monthly payments, times 4 years). Assume for the purpose of this example that the present value of $2,880 received monthly over the next four years is $2,400. The $2,400 exceeds 90% of the fair value of the lease at its inception. To calculate this, 90% of $2,500 equals $2,250. Since $2,400 exceeds $2,250, this criterion has been met and the lease would be classified as a capital lease.

Tip There are three factors that complicate this calculation. First, as you may have guessed, the question of what the lease term is must be addressed, and considerations such as those described above must be taken into account. Second, the calculation is based on the present value of the minimum lease payments. Minimum lease payments are those that the lessee is making or can be required to make in connection with the leased asset. Other factors, such as lease executory costs, guarantees of residual values, and any payments made for failure to extend or renew the lease may or may not have an impact on this amount, depending on the circumstances. Third, in order to determine the present value of the minimum lease payments, an appropriate interest (discount) rate must be determined. This rate is set at the incremental borrowing rate of the lessee, unless the interest rate implicit in the lease is known and is less than the not-for-profit organization's incremental borrowing rate. (The incremental borrowing rate is a fancy way of describing the interest rate that an organization would currently have to pay for a new debt instrument or similar obligation that would add to its current debt burden.) While the details of these factors are beyond the scope of this discussion, it is important for the reader to note that these factors enter into the calculations used to determine whether a lease is a capital lease.

To summarize the operating lease and capital lease determination methodology, if a lease meets one of the above criteria, it is considered a capital lease. Only one of the criteria needs to be met. If a lease does not meet *any* of the criteria described above, it is considered to be an operating lease.

OPERATING LEASES

Operating leases are the easiest leases to account for in the financial statements of a not-for-profit organization. Basically, in the case of a lessee, rent expense is charged in the period that it is incurred under the lease. (Leases with scheduled rent increases or free rent periods complicate this a little, but these issues are covered later in this chapter.)

Practical Example   A not-for-profit organization leases office space for $500 per month in a lease agreement that is properly accounted for as an operating lease. The not-for-profit organization would record a rent expense each month of $500, or, assuming that the lease covered the entire fiscal year at the same rent, $6,000 would be recorded as the annual office rent expense. If the not-for-profit organization was required to pay a security deposit to the owner at the inception of the lease and was entitled to receive this deposit back at the end of the lease, the amount paid as a security deposit would be recorded as an asset on the statement of financial position.

In an operating lease, there is no recognition of the leased asset itself in the statement of financial position, because the substance of the lease is a rental. There is no reason to expect that the lessee not-for-profit organization will derive any future economic benefit from the leased asset or incur the risks of ownership of the asset once the lease term has ended.

Lessors account for operating leases in much the same way, except rental income is recorded instead of rent expense.

Practical Example   Using the same facts as the above example, the lessor records $500 of rental income each month, or, with the same assumptions as above, $6,000 of rental income for the year.

Three additional considerations are made by a lessor in accounting for an operating lease:

- *First, in the lessor's statement of financial position, the leased asset remains recorded as an asset.* However, the asset should be captioned something like "Investment in leased property" and not included with the other amounts included in property, plant, and equipment. The leased property asset is depreciated by the lessor in the same manner as the lessor depreciates its other fixed assets.
- *Second, the lessor may incur costs at the start of the lease that relate specifically to the lease.* If the costs are insignificant, they can be charged to expense in the period incurred by the lessor. For example, if the only cost is a $500 legal fee for reviewing the lease agreement, it would be reasonable to charge this amount to expense in the year incurred. However, if the lessor had to make substantial improvements to the asset that is being leased, these amounts would be capitalized and amortized over the life of the lease.

Practical Example   Continuing with the above lease example, let us say that the lease term is 10 years. However, prior to the tenant (that is, the lessee) agreeing to enter into the lease, the lessor (owner) agreed to spend $5,000 on new carpeting and lighting for the office space that was being leased. The $5,000 would be recorded as an asset (a deferred charge) and amortized (that is, systematically charged to expense) over the 10-year life of the lease.

Assuming straight-line amortization is being used, expense would be charged for $500 each year ($5,000 divided by 10 years) and, correspondingly, the deferred charge asset would be reduced by $500 each year.

- *Finally, in the case of scheduled rent increases or free rent periods, the lessor follows an accounting for the lease similar to that of the lessee,* as will be described later in the chapter.

OPERATING LEASES WITH SCHEDULED RENT INCREASES

Rent expense recorded as a result of an operating lease is recognized on a straight-line basis over the term of the lease. In the examples for the lessee and lessor provided above, this is a simple calculation since the amount of the monthly rental is fixed at $500. If a lease contains a scheduled rent increase, the total amount of the payments made (in the case of the lessee) or received (in the case of the lessor) are allocated over the entire term of the lease.

Practical Example   Assume that an operating lease is entered into for office space for three years. The rents are fixed as follows:

Year 1	$500 per month	$6,000 per year
Year 2	$600 per month	$7,200 per year
Year 3	$700 per month	$8,400 per year

The total rent expense for the lessee under this lease is $21,600 ($6,000 plus $7,200 plus $8,400) over the three-year period. The lessee does *not* charge $6,000 to expense in Year 1, $7,200 in Year 2, and $8,400 in Year 3, as one might expect. Rather, rent expense is calculated by taking the total rents due under the lease ($21,600) and dividing it by the three-year lease payment to obtain the amount of $7,200, which is the amount charged to expense by the lessee in each of the three years covered by the lease term. In Year 1, the lessee only pays $6,000, yet records an expense of $7,200, meaning that $1,200 must be recorded as an accrued liability under the lease and recorded in the statement of financial position. In this simple example, in Year 2, the amount of the payment ($7,200) equals the amount of the expense, so no accrued expense entries are needed. In Year 3, a payment is made of $8,400, yet an expense is charged for only $7,200. The difference ($1,200) reduces the accrued liability and brings this account to zero, which is appropriate, since Year 3 is the end of the lease term.

The lessor would perform similar calculations in this example, except that in Year 1 it would record a receivable for the $1,200 difference between the rental income earned and the amount of cash received. In Year 2, the amount of rental income earned would equal the amount of cash received as rent. In Year 3, when the amount received is $1,200 greater than the amount of rental income earned, this difference is credited to the receivable, which reduces it to zero, appropriately so, since Year 3 is the end of the lease term.

FREE RENT PERIODS

Sometimes as an inducement for a lessee to enter into a lease agreement, the lessor (owner) will offer the lessee a free rent period at the beginning of the lease. Free rent periods are most popular in leases of office space. In times of a very tight commercial real estate rental market, free rent declines in popularity as landlords are able to rent space without the benefit of this inducement. On the other hand, when the market for commercial real estate rental becomes softer, the popularity of free rent inducements increases.

In the above example, for instance, the lessee may be given the inducement of not having to pay any rent for the first three months of the lease. The concept for the above calculation would remain the same. In calculating the total rents to be paid under the lease, Year 1 would include only nine months of actual rent payments, or $4,500. Added to the subsequent years' payments of $7,200 and $8,400, the total payment to be made under the lease becomes $20,100. Accordingly, the amount of annual expense recorded under the lease becomes $20,100 divided by the three-year lease term, or $6,700 each year. Note that the accrued liability account would be handled the same way.

The lessor's (owner's) accounting for free rent periods works the same way and is the mirror image of that described for the accounting for lessees.

CAPITAL LEASES

Accounting for capital leases resembles an actual sale and purchase of an asset, rather than a lease. The specific accounting issues relating to capital leases are described in this section.

Lessee Accounting

The following discussion describes the accounting treatment that should be used by a lessee in recording a lease that has been identified as a capital lease. Again, the essence of the transaction is that the risks and rewards of ownership of the asset are, in substance, transferred to the lessee. Accordingly, the lessee records the leased property as an asset and records a liability to reflect its ongoing obligation to make payments under the lease.

Using the guidance of SFAS 13, the lessee records a capital lease by recording a capital asset and a liability at an amount equal to the present value of the minimum lease payments at the beginning of the lease. The amounts recorded, however, should not exceed the fair value of the leased asset.

Referring back to the section of this chapter that covers determining whether a lease is a capital lease, the calculation of the amount of the asset and liability recorded when recording a capital lease contains three factors which are not always clear-cut. These are:

- Minimum lease payments
- Lease term
- Discount rate to be used for purposes of calculating present value

Realistically speaking, a non-accountant would not be expected to perform the calculations for recording a capital lease. In attempting to understand what has been recorded by a not-for-profit organization, the non-accountant might find the following discussion of the individual factors to be considered when a capital lease is recorded by a lessee to be useful.

For purposes of computing the amount of the asset and liability to be recorded, the minimum lease payments are considered to be the payments that the lessee is obligated to make or can be required to make. This would exclude costs such as insurance, maintenance, and taxes. The minimum lease payments generally include the minimum rental payments, any guarantee of the residual value made by the lessee for the asset at the end of the lease term, and the penalty for failure to renew the lease, if applicable. If the lease includes a bargain purchase option, the amount required to be paid under this option is also included in the minimum lease payments.

The present value of the minimum lease payments is computed using the incremental borrowing rate (described earlier in this chapter) of the lessee unless it is practicable for the lessee to determine the implicit rate computed by the lessor. In order for the implicit rate to be used, it must be less than the incremental borrowing rate.

The lease term used in determining the present value is the fixed, noncancelable term of the lease increased by any or all of the following:

- All periods covered by bargain renewal options
- All periods for which failure to renew imposes a penalty on the lessee
- All periods covered by ordinary renewal options during

which the lessee guarantees the lessor's debt on the leased property

- All periods covered by ordinary renewals or extensions up to the date a bargain purchase option is exercisable
- All periods representing renewals or extensions of the lease at the lessor's option

If the amount computed as the present value of the minimum lease payments exceeds the fair value of the leased property at the inception of the lease, the amount recorded should be that of the fair value of the leased property.

The amortization of the leased asset will depend on how the lease qualified as a capital lease. If the lease transaction met the criteria as either transferring ownership or containing a bargain purchase option (criteria 1 or 2 listed earlier in this chapter), then the asset arising from the transaction is to be amortized over the estimated useful life of the leased property. If the transaction qualifies as a capital lease because it met either the 75% of useful life or 90% of fair market value (criteria 3 or 4 listed earlier in this chapter), the asset must be amortized over the lease term. The reason for this difference arises because of the substance of the transaction. Under the first two criteria, the asset actually becomes the property of the lessee at the end of the lease term (or upon exercise of the bargain purchase option). In the latter situations, the title to the property remains with the lessor.

The leased asset is to be amortized (depreciated) over the lease term if title does not transfer to the lessee, while the asset is depreciated in a manner consistent with the lessee's normal depreciation policy if the title is to eventually transfer to the lessee. This latter situation can be interpreted to mean that the asset is depreciated over the useful economic life of the leased asset. The treatment and method used to amortize (depreciate) the leased asset is very similar to that used for any other asset. The amortization entry requires a debit to the lease expense and a credit to an accumulated amortization account. The leased asset should not be amortized below the estimated residual value.

In some instances when the property is to revert back to the lessor, there may be a guaranteed residual value. This is an amount which the lessee guarantees to the lessor. If the fair market value of the asset at the end of the lease term is greater than or equal to the guaranteed residual amount, the lessee incurs no additional obligation. On the other hand, if the fair market value of the leased asset is less than the guaranteed residual value, then the lessee must make up the difference, usually with a cash payment. The guaranteed residual value is often used as a tool to reduce the periodic payments by substituting the lump-sum amount at the end of the term which results from the guarantee. In any event, the amortization must still take place based on the estimated residual value. This results in a rational and systematic allocation of the expense through the periods and avoids a large loss (or expense) in the last period as a result of the guarantee.

The annual (periodic) rent payments made during the lease term are to be allocated between a reduction in the liability that is recorded at the inception of the lease and interest expense. The calculation of the split of the periodic rental payment between the repayment of the liability and interest expense is made by something called the *effective interest method*. While this sounds complex, it is simply a technique used to reflect the fact that as the obligation is paid back over the term of the lease, there is really less of an interest cost relating to the outstanding liability, since the liability is decreasing. Accordingly, using the effective interest method, as the lease progresses, more of the lease payments are allocated to the reduction of the liability and less is allocated to interest expense. This is a concept that homeowners should be familiar with, since it is not unlike the allocation of a monthly mortgage payment between principal and interest over the life of the mortgage.

Lessor Accounting

This section will present the fundamentals of how a lessor would account for a capital lease. Note, however, that in the vast majority of real-life situations a not-for-profit organization is going to be the lessee and not the lessor under a capital lease.

As with the lessee, the first step for the lessor is to determine whether or not the lease is a capital lease. Conceptually, the lessor will record a receivable (representing its interest in the future payments to be received under the lease) and will remove the asset that it has leased from its statement of financial position. The lessor's classification of a capital lease is further classified into three types of capital leases. These types are:

- Sales-type leases
- Direct financing leases
- Leveraged leases

In those cases where a not-for-profit organization is the lessor in a capital lease transaction, it is likely that the lease will be accounted for as a direct financing lease. Accordingly, that type of capital lease is the focus of the following discussion.

In a direct financing lease, the fair market value of the leased item and the cost of the recorded asset are the same, so that there is no gain or loss recognized on the actual lease transaction. (In a sales-type capital lease, a manufacturer's profit would be recognized as part of the lease transaction.) The profit to the lessor in a direct financing lease is the interest revenue earned as a result of the lease. The lessor records an asset for the net investment in the lease, which basically represents the present value of the future minimum lease payments. The gross investment in the lease (total of the payments to be received) is compared with the net investment in the lease (basically the present value of the future minimum lease payments) and the difference is unearned interest income. As the lease progresses, the unearned interest income amount is realized as interest income on the lease using a method similar to the effective interest method described earlier. Essentially, the lessor's asset is replaced with a long-term receivable, part of which represents interest income that will be recognized over the term of the lease. The computations are also affected by items such as guaranteed residual values and initial direct costs under the leases, but these are beyond the scope of this overview.

SUMMARY

Once again, a reasonably complex area of accounting can best be understood by focusing on the fundamentals of the transaction that is being recorded. In the case of accounting for leases, the first determination is whether or not the lease is a simple rental (operating lease) or whether the risks and rewards of ownership pass, in substance, to the lessee, making the transaction more of a sale of an asset than a rental (capital lease). A capital lease results in the actual recording of the asset being leased by the lessee and the asset being removed from the books of the lessor. Keeping these simple concepts in mind should make understanding how a not-for-profit organization has accounted for its lease transactions much clearer.

CHAPTER 11

Analyzing the Financial Health of Not-for-Profit Organizations

Hopefully, reading the previous chapters of this book has piqued the interest of the non-accountant in the importance of accounting and financial information to not-for-profit organizations. Sometimes individuals believe that accounting and finance are not important for not-for-profit organizations since their primary mission is not to make money, but to pursue whatever is the exempt function—their reason for being. Many donors and certainly all lenders and other creditors to not-for-profit organizations probably could not disagree more. They are keenly interested in the accounting and finances of not-for-profit organizations. The members of the board of directors of a not-for-profit organization and the nonfinancial management of a not-for-profit organization sometimes do not focus on the many users of a not-for-profit organization's financial statements and other financial information. For instance, consider these users of not-for-profit financial information:

- *Donors* (although they may not express this explicitly, particularly smaller donors) are interested in knowing whether their contribution of assets to the not-for-profit organization is being used effectively and not squandered.
- *Grantors and other contractors* are interested in knowing that

their funding to the not-for-profit organization is being used for the purpose for which it was intended. They are interested in knowing whether all of the assets (money) given to the not-for-profit organization have been used, what these resources have been spent on, and whether the resources have been spent in compliance with the applicable grant agreement or contract that was executed with the not-for-profit organization.

- *Lenders* to not-for-profit organizations have an interest in determining whether a not-for-profit organization can repay amounts borrowed, regardless of whether the borrowing is a short-term loan or a long-term loan secured by a mortgage.
- *Vendors and other service providers* are interested in knowing whether a not-for-profit organization has the financial resources to pay its bills on a timely basis.
- *Employees* are interested in knowing whether the not-for-profit organization has the resources to continue in existence, to have resources for salaries and other employee benefits, whether the organization is growing or contracting, and the effect of that growth or contraction on advancement opportunities. Employees are also interested in knowing whether the organization will be in a position in the future to provide an adequate level of compensation and fringe benefits that would make long-term employment at the not-for-profit organization desirable.
- *Government regulators,* including state charities bureaus and the Internal Revenue Service, are interested in knowing whether appropriate financial information is being made available to the public. The Internal Revenue Service is interested in any for-profit activities of not-for-profit organizations as well as any unrelated business income that is being generated by these organizations.

Given that the financial statements and other financial information is so important, a non-accountant might ask: "OK, I'm reading the financial statements of a not-for-profit organization for which I have just been appointed to the board of directors. What am I supposed to be looking for?" This chapter helps to answer that question by suggesting some areas that can be looked at, provides a number of calculations that can be performed for financial analysis, and suggests that an analysis of budget to actual performance, if available, can be very useful in financial analysis.

The following section of this chapter will cover some of the financial indicators that can be obtained from the financial statements. The last section of this chapter will review how a not-for-profit organization can be analyzed by looking at its budgeting process.

So, if those financial statements that you are looking at are part of a beautifully prepared, glossy annual report, look past all of those wonderful pictures and the heartfelt letter of the executive director and skip to the back, where the financial statements are usually buried, pull out your magnifying glass to cope with the microscopic type size, and look for some of the following information.

FINANCIAL STATEMENT ANALYSIS

The following items should be very helpful in understanding the financial health of a not-for-profit organization. Keep in mind that all not-for-profit organizations are different and a combination of these and other indicators might be important to understand their financial health. In addition, keep in mind that not-for-profit organizations operate in a variety of different "industries" (for example, voluntary health organizations, colleges, health-care providers, civic associations, country clubs, etc.), each of which has its own unique operating characteristics that affect financial analysis.

INDEPENDENT AUDITOR'S REPORT

The first item to read in the financial statements is the independent auditor's report. Look for a standard three-paragraph report that indicates that the financial statements are prepared in accordance with GAAP and that the audit was performed in accordance with generally accepted auditing standards (GAAS). There may be an additional paragraph to the report stating whether the auditor applied any auditing procedures to any supplementary information that accompanies the basic financial statements. This is generally no cause for alarm.

The independent auditor's report, however, may be modified to report circumstances which should be of interest to the reader of a not-for-profit organization's financial statements. The independent auditor's report may note one or more departures from GAAP, such as: "The financial statements are in accordance with GAAP, except for . . ." (with a description of the GAAP exception), or may indicate that because of some restrictions to the scope of their audit, their opinion is qualified: " . . . subject to any adjustments that might have been identified had the audit procedures been performed." These qualifications are red flags that should caution the reader to find out about the reasons for these problems and why they could not be resolved between the not-for-profit organization and its auditor.

Tip   In some cases, the qualification may make sense and not be cause for alarm. For example, if the auditor has a scope limitation because he or she is unable to observe an inventory of supplies and equipment maintained by a research organization at the South Pole for a financial statement audit for a fiscal year ended June 30, there is less assurance about the recorded amounts of the supplies and the equipment. However, it does make some sense that an auditor could not go to the South Pole during June to observe that inventory. It does not appear that the not-for-profit organization precluded the auditor from doing some procedure that the auditor wanted to perform. On the other hand, if the scope exception is that the not-for-profit organization refused to allow the auditor to confirm receivables from donors and other fee-for-service revenue providers, the financial statement reader should be more skeptical of why the not-for-profit organization prevented the auditor from performing these procedures.

In some instances, the departures from GAAP or limitations in the scope of the audit may be so important that modifying the standard auditor's report is not sufficient to communicate the seriousness of the problem. In severe instances where a departure from GAAP is pervasive to the financial statements, the auditor might issue an adverse opinion, indicating that the financial statements as a whole are not prepared in accordance with GAAP. If the scope limitation in an audit is very severe or pervasive, an auditor might issue a disclaimer of opinion, which indicates that the auditor is unable to give any assurance at all on the financial statements. These are very red flags that indicate that there may be some real problems with the financial statements.

The independent auditor's report might also indicate that a different level of engagement was conducted by the independent auditor. Each of the following is an example of the modifications to the types of procedures performed and the level of assurance provided:

- *Compilation.* This is a very limited type of engagement where an auditor basically takes information from the not-for-profit organization's financial reports and prepares financial statements from those records. The auditor offers no level of assurance on the amounts reported in the financial statements. Sometimes the management of a not-for-profit organization may elect to omit the disclosures that are normally made in the notes to the financial statements when the auditor only performs a compilation of the financial statements.
- *Review.* This is also a limited type of engagement where the auditor does much less work than in an audit in accordance with GAAS, yet *does* perform certain inquiries and financial statement analysis to provide a very limited form of

assurance on the financial statements. While a review engagement may be viewed as being between a compilation and an audit, it is much closer in scope to a compilation than it is to an audit.

Tip   Having an auditor perform a compilation or review of the financial statements should not automatically be viewed negatively because the scope of these procedures is far less than an audit. In some cases, particularly for small not-for-profit organizations, these types of engagements may be used to satisfy state or local financial reporting requirements. They are also usually far less costly than an audit and, depending on the circumstances, may be adequate for the not-for-profit organization's needs.

- *Audit in accordance with Government Auditing Standards (GAS).* If the not-for-profit organization is subject to the federal Single Audit requirements because it is a recipient of resources under federal awards programs, the auditor performs an audit in accordance with the Single Audit requirements as well as GAS. The standards for GAS are set by the Comptroller General of the United States. The auditor's opinion on the basic financial statements usually indicates whether it was performed in accordance with GAS. The auditor also issues a report on internal control and compliance with laws and regulations relating to the preparation of the financial statements. An audit performed in accordance with GAS does not require the auditor to perform any significant additional procedures than an audit performed in accordance with GAAS, although GAS does contain certain standards and requirements to which an auditor must adhere. For example, there are specific continuing education requirements that an auditor performing an audit in accordance with GAS must meet. There is no similar requirement in GAAS (although auditors who are members of the AICPA have different continuing education requirements).

COMPARATIVE FINANCIAL STATEMENTS

One of the very basic methods used to look at financial statements analytically is to compare the current year amounts with the prior year amounts. Usually, financial statements are prepared on a comparative basis, meaning both the current year and the prior year information is presented. Although GAAP encourage comparative financial statements to be presented, they do not require it. For not-for-profit organizations, sometimes only summarized comparative information for the prior year is presented, rather than full comparative financial statements for both years. Not-for-profit organizations got into the practice of presenting only summarized prior year financial information when the requirements of fund accounting caused one year's financial statements to spread out over more than one page. The switch to net asset classifications has helped reduce this financial statement spread, but information about net asset classification and functional reporting also makes current not-for-profit financial statements conducive to only report-summarized prior year data.

In comparing two years of financial information, the reader might first look for significant differences in amounts from one year to the next and try to find out the reasons for these differences. Calculating the differences as a percentage of the prior year amounts might also shed some light on the analysis, since large dollar differences might not be significant if they are differences in amounts that are themselves large in relation to the other amounts reported in the financial statements.

Another interesting technique is to look for line items with amounts that did not exist in the prior year, but do exist in the current year. Conversely, line items with amounts in the prior year with no amounts in the current year might also provide some interesting information. This analysis may provide important information about the operations of a not-for-profit organization during its fiscal year.

Let us say that a not-for-profit organization had no short-term borrowings as of the year-end of the prior year, but does have short-term borrowings at the end of the current year. Does this mean that the organization was strapped for cash and had to obtain short-term financing or tap into a line of credit in the current year? Does the short-term borrowing relate to a new program that did not exist in the prior year? Answers to these questions can tell a lot about the financial condition of the not-for-profit organization.

Since we know from Chapter 4 that a not-for-profit organization's investments in most equities and all debt instruments are recorded at fair value, what is the difference in the investment amount from the prior year to the current year? Does the amount make sense in light of the stock market changes and the changes in interest rates during the year? Check the statement of cash flows to see if there have been significant purchases and sales of investments that also might affect these year-end balances.

Other questions that may be asked in comparing the two years of financial information are:

- Have significant investments in property, plant, and equipment been made during the year?
- Has long-term and short-term debt increased or decreased?
- Has contribution revenue increased or decreased? Does the recorded contribution receivable balance correspond to significant fluctuations in contribution revenue?
- Did revenues exceed expenditures (or vice versa) in the current year, and is this consistent with the prior year?
- Is the level of fee-for-service activities' revenues consistent with the prior year? Can large fluctuations be explained?
- Are expenses, including program, management and general, and fund-raising, consistent with the prior year? Can large fluctuations be explained?
- Did overall net assets increase or decrease from the prior year? What is the amount of unrestricted net assets, and has this amount increased or decreased from the prior year?

These are but a few of the questions that might come to mind in comparing two years' worth of financial information. Also useful is to try to see if the financial statements reflect significant events that the reader knows occurred in the current year. For example, if the not-for-profit organization opened a new facility, fired half of its staff, increased salaries by 10%, or obtained a new federal grant program, could the effect of these events in the current year be discerned in comparing the prior year financial statements with the current year's? It is important not only to focus on what is recorded in the financial statements but also to test whether what should be recorded in the financial statements is properly recorded.

FUNCTIONAL EXPENSE RATIOS AND OTHER ANALYSES

As described in Chapter 2, a not-for-profit organization's statement of activities reports expenses in their functional classifications:

- Program expenses
- Management and general expenses
- Fund-raising expenses
- Membership development expenses (for membership organizations)

The following are some useful analyses that can be used to gauge a not-for-profit organization's performance. For each of these analyses, comparing the calculation with the prior year or years and comparing the specific not-for-profit organization to other not-for-profit organizations in similar fields, with similar structures, can be very effective.

Ratio of Program Expenses to Total Expenses

Not-for-profit organizations exist not to make money, but to spend money on their "exempt function," which essentially represents the reason for their existence. Dividing an organization's program expenses by its total expenses provides an indication of how much of an organization's total operations are spent on the programs for which it exists. Generally, the higher this percentage, the better. This percentage tells a perspective donor how much of their $1 contribution can be expected to be used for program activities, which are generally the reason the donor is making the contribution in the first place. Many organizations try to spend 75% to 80% of their total expenses on program activities. This ratio is one of the most important performance indicators for not-for-profit organizations and is one that is of particular interest to current and potential donors.

However, keep in mind that all not-for-profit organizations do need administrative and fund-raising operations that cost money. It is possible to spend too little money on administration and fund-raising to the long-term detriment of the organization's ability to continue in existence. Comparing the calculated percentage with prior years and with other organizations can be very helpful.

Ratio of Management and General Expenses to Total Expenses

Dividing the total management and general expenses by total expenses results in a percentage that indicates how much of every dollar spent by an organization is spent on administrative activities. This ratio can be very sensitive to the size of the organization. Very small not-for-profit organizations may have a relatively high ratio of management and general expenses to total expenses because even one or two employees with an office can result in a relatively high level of expenses given the size of very small not-for-profit organizations. Again, while a low percentage is deemed desirable, not-for-profit organizations *do* need to maintain a certain level of administrative activities to continue to exist.

Ratio of Fund-raising Expenses to Total Expenses

Dividing fund-raising expenses by total expenses results in a percentage that indicates how much of each dollar spent by the not-for-profit organization is spent to raise money. While current and potential donors may understand that a certain part of the money that they contribute will go to program activities and a certain part to administering the organization and those programs, it is perhaps less thrilling to them to know how much of each dollar that the organization spends of their contributions simply goes to raising more money. Nevertheless, fund-raising *is* an important function of not-for-profit organizations, and allocating too few resources to fund-raising can have very detrimental long-term impacts on a not-for-profit organization.

Tip   From purely anecdotal evidence of reading financial statements of not-for-profit organizations, it seems that the amount of fund-raising expenses is often understated in the financial statements. The author has seen financial statements of not-for-profit organizations with significant contribution revenue levels with no fund-raising expenses being reported. This is counterintuitive. It is likely that these expenses are being treated as management and general expenses, because in the absence of a formal fund-raising department, many fund-raising activities are performed by management. Before applauding one organization over another for its low percentage of fund-raising expenses, the reader of the financial statements might inquire about how such expenses are actually allocated. For instance, if the executive director of the organization spends 25% of his or her time on fund-raising activities, is an allocation of the cost of that time being made by the organization and reported as fund-raising expenses?

Ratio of Contribution Revenues to Fund-raising Expenses

To compute this ratio, take the contributions revenue reported by the not-for-profit organization in the statement of activities and divide that amount by the fund-raising expenses for the same period. This performance indicator measures how much money is raised for each dollar spent on fund-raising. Obviously, the higher the ratio, the better.

To really understand the efficiency of a fund-raising program, however, the reader may have to analyze the components of this ratio more carefully. Consider some of the factors that may influence this calculation:

- *Some contribution revenue may be the result of fund-raising efforts of prior years,* for example, if a donor agreed five years ago to contribute $1 million a year for the next ten years. Assume that the donor attached some conditions to this contribution that prevented it all from being recognized as contribution revenue (with a related receivable) in the year that the promise to give was made. In this example, the current year would have virtually no fund-raising costs related to this contribution, but would have the benefit of the $1 million of contribution revenue. Assuming that whatever conditions the donor imposed are met, contribution revenue is recognized for the $1 million. The $1 million of revenue (with no related expenses) might make the current year's fund-raising activities seem efficient, but the revenue is really the result of prior year efforts.

- *Some current fund-raising efforts may result in expenses in the current period with the benefit not occurring until future years.* Continuing with the above example, the fund-raising efforts for a contribution occurring five years ago may have started one or two years before the contribution was made. These two years prior to the contribution had no contribution revenue to show in the year that the costs were incurred, but they resulted in a total of $10 million in contributions in future years.

- *Different types of fund-raising activities are expected to have different returns.* For example, the executive director may have· a few meetings with the head of a corporate-giving program at a major corporation, which result in a significant contribution to the not-for-profit organization with very little relative cost. On the other hand, mass direct mailings to thousands of potential donors often are very expensive to accomplish and may not produce a very high response rate.

These factors do not indicate that the computed ratio is not useful. First, it may cause the analyst to ask questions, whose responses may lead to valuable information about the efficiency of the fund-raising department. Second, viewing the trend in the ratio over a longer period of time, such as five or ten years, will tend to even out some of the year-to-year fluctuations. In addition, this long-term perspective will highlight trends in the direction that the efficiency of the fund-raising effort is headed.

Reading a Not-for-Profit Organization's Bottom Line

Many of the financial indicators for commercial enterprises focus on net income (or, in some cases, net income and comprehensive income). The net increase or decrease in unrestricted net assets of a not-for-profit organization is approximately what could be considered its net income, or results from operations. Unlike a for-profit company, however, more is generally not better when it comes to this performance indicator.

Not-for-profit organizations, as their name suggests, are supposed to spend their resources on the program activities and supporting services, not to earn a profit. A very small increase or decrease in unrestricted net assets is generally what should be expected by the financial statement reader. Many not-for-profit organizations work hard to maintain this balancing act of keeping their expenses in line with their revenues, although, like other businesses, this is not always feasible in any given year.

There may be circumstances where the not-for-profit organization is attempting to accumulate resources for future use, such as a major building program. It might try to run a "profit" for a few years to accumulate resources for some longer-term purpose. On the other hand (and rarer), the not-for-profit organization may feel that it has too many resources. Perhaps it received an unexpected windfall gift from a donor in one year that it is spending over a period of several years. In the subsequent years of this gift, it would decrease its unrestricted net assets as it spends down the one year's unexpected gift.

One might wonder what is so wrong with a not-for-profit organization steadily improving its financial position by consistently having a net increase in net assets each year. There are at least two answers to this. First, as alluded to earlier, donors contribute to not-for-profit organizations not because they want the organization to hoard their money, but because they want the organization to spend their money on the organization's exempt purpose, which we have been referring to as its reason for being.

Second, particularly for larger donors, not-for-profit organizations need to make a "case statement," which describes for the donor why it is important for them to contribute to the not-for-profit organization. Which is a better case statement: "We need your $100,000 contribution because we are in desperate financial straits and without your contribution we will have to suspend our program of shipping food to starving children in the XYZ country" or "We are trying to build a rock-solid not-for-profit organization and your $100,000 will help both management and the board of directors sleep better at night"? While sometimes donors are admittedly leery of donating to financially unstable organizations, the immediacy of the need in the first case statement is far more likely to result in contributions than the second. Stated simply, donors are likely to be less inclined to contribute more to a not-for-profit organization that is already not spending as much of the assets that it has at its disposal as it can.

Reliance on a Limited Number of Revenue Sources

The financial statement reader should look at the various revenue sources to get a sense of whether the organization is highly dependent on one or two sources of revenue that might present a risk to its operations should these revenue sources cease to exist. This risk concentration is important because there is no assurance that a not-for-profit organization could easily and quickly replace the revenue source. If there are not sufficient assets in reserve for use in such occasions, the financial viability of the not-for-profit organization could diminish rapidly.

These revenue sources may first be broken down into their basic types: contributions from donors, fee-for-service activities, contracts or grants from governmental agencies, and others. These basic revenue sources can be further analyzed to determine if one or more of the following characteristics is putting the not-for-profit organization at risk:

- *Contributions from donors*
  - High percentage of contributions coming from one or two specific donors
  - Large concentration of donors in a particular industry or geographic location
  - Competition for donors from a new or newly active not-for-profit organization with a similar mission targeting similar potential donor groups
- *Fee-for-service activities*
  - Existence of one or two large contracts for services (day-care services, home health-care workers, etc.) that account for a large percentage of total fee-for-service revenues
  - Competition from similar organizations for the primary fee-for-service activities performed
  - Declining student enrollment or hospital admissions that result in steady decreases in a primary revenue source
- *Grants or contracts from governmental agencies and others*
  - Reliance on grants or contracts from one or two private foundations
  - Reliance on a government contract or grant from one or two sources, including federal, state, or local governments
  - Dependence on government grants that are subject to annual appropriations from the government

Not all of these situations indicate that the not-for-profit organization is on the brink of financial catastrophe. It does mean, however, that there is a risk to the not-for-profit organization that a significant revenue source may end or diminish.

Renewable Revenue Sources

In looking at a not-for-profit organization's sources of revenue, there is one perspective that is useful is determining how much of the total revenue comes in somewhat routinely and how much has to be fought for periodically by the organization. Consider these two extremes:

- A not-for-profit organization that sponsors a local soccer club for neighborhood children uses a variety of methods to raise contributions of small dollar amounts from collection canisters placed in local retail shops, door-to-door solicitations, sponsoring a neighborhood 5K race, and running car washes. Its contributions are small, raised from a variety of sources, and have a variety of different types of donors. While some years' contributions will be better than others, the revenues will be more or less steady from year to year and are easy to renew because there is a large number of potential donors and the donors are only asked for relatively small contributions.

- A research-oriented not-for-profit organization obtains 90% of its revenues from a federal grant to conduct a specific type of research. Every three years, the not-for-profit organization has to compete with five other similar organizations to retain this grant. Clearly, loss of renewal of this grant would have a severe impact on the financial health of the not-for-profit organization. In this case, the not-for-profit organization not only has the problem of being dependent on one federal agency as the source of its funds, but also the renewal of those funds every three years intensifies the risk that the funding under this grant will be lost.

While perhaps extreme, these examples highlight circumstances where easily renewable resources can be far less risky to an organization than the situation where the organization bets its very existence every three years when it submits its proposal to continue to receive its lifeblood grant.

Liquidity and Other Financial Indicators

There are a number of ratios and other financial indicators that are used for not-for-profit organizations, as well as commercial enterprises, to indicate whether or not the organization is financially healthy. A number of these ratios and financial indicators involve profitability and do not apply to not-for-profit organizations (with the exception of instances where they operate for-profit activities). Some of the more common financial ratios and indicators are described below:

Working Capital

A not-for-profit organization's working capital is equal to the excess of its current assets over its current liabilities. (Recall from Chapter 2 that some organizations may not present a classified balance sheet, meaning that performing this, and several other ratios, will require some work on the part of the financial analyst.) The amount of working capital is an indication of how much of short-term financial resources will be left over if all of the organization's short-term financial obligations are paid off. Generally, the more, the better. However, excessive amounts of working capital may indicate that the organization might be better off making longer-term investments or perhaps paying off longer-term debt. Viewing trends in the amount of working capital over several years provides an indication of whether short-term financial health is improving or deteriorating. Keep in mind that care should be taken not to include donor or other restricted assets in the current asset amount where these would not be available to liquidate current liabilities.

Current Ratio

The current ratio is similar in purpose to the calculation of working capital. The current ratio is computed by dividing the current assets by the current liabilities. It provides, in terms that are relative to the size of the current assets and liabilities, how many times over the not-for-profit organization can pay its current liabilities with its current assets. Again, trends are important, as is consideration of the fact that any short-term assets that are restricted are not available to pay current liabilities.

Quick Ratio

A variation of the current ratio that provides more information about current assets that are more readily convertible to cash is the quick ratio. This is calculated the same way as the current ratio, except that, instead of current assets, only those current assets most readily convertible to cash are included, which would include cash and cash equivalents, short-term investments, and receivables.

Debt Ratio

This ratio divides the amount of debt outstanding by total assets. For a not-for-profit organization, unrestricted assets may be a more appropriate measure, depending on whether any temporarily restricted assets are available to pay for debt service. This ratio provides an indication of how much of a not-for-profit organization's assets are financed by the issuance of debt. It also provides a measure of the level of assets that would be available to pay off debt in the event of liquidation. The problem with viewing the ratio this way is that the liquidation value of the assets may be lower, or much lower, than their recorded book value.

Receivables Turnover

This ratio can be applied to both receivables from fee-for-service activities and contributions receivable, although a separate calculation for each is probably more effective. Revenue (either fee-for-service or contribution) is divided by the average outstanding balance of receivables (either fee-for-service or contribution). The average receivable balance is calculated by adding the beginning of the year and end of the year balances and then dividing by two.

This ratio provides a rough indication of the amount of time that it takes to turn receivables into cash. For example, if the receivables turnover ratio is calculated at 4, the average age of the receivables is 91 days (365 days divided by 4). A high average age of receivables might indicate that they are not being collected fast enough to provide the cash needed to finance current operations. It may also be indicative of a collectibility problem with the receivables. Note that the average days outstanding will likely consist of some receivables that are collected very quickly, while others may be outstanding for a long period of time. In other words, there still may be some very old and uncollectible receivables in the outstanding receivables balances even if the overall number of days outstanding balance is reasonable.

Inventory Turnover

When a not-for-profit organization has inventory held for sale, it may be useful to calculate the inventory turnover ratio, which is similar in concept to the receivables turnover ratio. It is calculated by dividing the cost of goods sold (reported on the statement of activities and representing the cost of the inventory sold during the year) by the average inventory balance. The average inventory balance is computed by adding the beginning of the year inventory balance with the end of the year balance and then dividing by two. This ratio gives a rough indication of how long it takes to sell an item of inventory. For example, if the ratio is computed as five, it takes roughly 73 days to sell an item from inventory (365 days divided by 5). This ratio can help to highlight slow-moving inventory that may be difficult to sell without discounting and may point to concerns about whether the inventory is recorded at the lower of its cost or market value. As with receivables, quickly selling inventory items may mask older inventory items, meaning that old inventory items may exist even if the number of days to sell an item appears reasonable.

BUDGET CONSIDERATIONS IN
FINANCIAL ANALYSIS

The preceding discussion is based principally on the financial information generally found in the financial statements of not-for-profit organizations. Some non-accountant "insiders" of not-for-profit organizations (such as members of management and the board of directors) not only have access to a physically prepared budget for the organization but probably participate in the budgeting process. The final part of this chapter describes the reasons why budgeting is so important to not-for-profit organizations and presents ideas for making this process a more effective financial analytical tool.

Importance of Budgets to Not-for-Profit Organizations

Budgets are generally more important to not-for-profit organizations than to commercial enterprises because a not-for-profit organization's budget is a blueprint of how it expects to use its limited resources to further its programmatic mission. While it is nice for a commercial organization to have a budget that anticipates a profit increase of, say, 10% from the previous year, if that organization achieves a 5% or 25% profit growth, the basic financial foundation of the organization is not dramatically impacted. (Although the stock price of the company and some management bonuses are likely to be affected.) On the other hand, if a not-for-profit organization misses its budgeted projections by a large amount, it could find itself in serious financial difficulties. As mentioned earlier in this chapter, not-for-profit organizations usually plan to break even each year, meaning that increases in unrestricted net assets equal decreases in unrestricted net assets. This is a very small target to aim for and many times not-for-profits do not have large accumulated financial cushions to soften the impact of budget overruns.

RELATION OF THE BUDGET TO
THE FINANCIAL STATEMENTS

It has sometimes seemed to the author that not-for-profit organizations have a disconnect in relating their budget to their financial statements. Management seems to focus on the budgeted amounts during the year, which is appropriate, but when it comes to the financial statements, management sometimes seems to just hope for the best and not manage these amounts. This may be caused by budgets sometimes being prepared on one basis of accounting, such as the cash basis, while the financial statements that are prepared in accordance with GAAP are on another basis of accounting, the accrual basis. Sometimes, even though the same basis of accounting is used for the budget and the financial statements, certain revenues and/or expenses are included in the financial statements but omitted from the budget calculation. Depreciation expense is a good example, as is the increase or decrease in net assets resulting from unrealized gains or losses, respectively, from investments. The key point is that if the management of the not-for-profit organization is preparing a budget based on something other than GAAP-based accrual accounting, the financial results for the fiscal year reported in the financial statements may vary widely from what was budgeted. In other words, if a budget is prepared on a cash basis and the budget indicates that the not-for-profit organization will break even for the year (increases in unrestricted net assets equal decreases in unrestricted net assets), you cannot necessarily expect that the financial statements will show that the organization broke even. The reason will not be that the actual amounts differed from the budgeted amounts (this is another problem that will be discussed later), but that the organization in this example is comparing apples (cash-based budget) to oranges (accrual-based financial statements).

Other such types of differences may arise because of what is included in the budget. Some organizations may elect to treat permanently and temporarily restricted net assets (and their increases and decreases during the year) separately from unrestricted net assets. Other organizations may have one budget that does not distinguish between the different classifications of net assets.

The remedy to this problem may not be difficult to formulate. If the budget is viewed as the plan that drives the organization to the actual results reported in the financial statements, differences such as those discussed above must be addressed. The not-for-profit organization simply either needs to budget on an accrual basis or take the adjustments typically needed to convert from the budget basis to the GAAP-based financial statements into consideration when preparing the budget. This will be possible for some items, such as depreciation. However, for items such as unrealized gains and losses on investments, this will be impossible to predict at the time the budget is prepared. On the other hand, if the not-for-profit organization does not view the budget as the document that drives its financial statement results (or is not overly concerned with its reported financial statement results), then the reconciliation of the budget to the financial statements will not be important to these organizations and is likely not to be addressed.

METHODS OF BUDGETARY CONTROL

Certainly the use of the budget as a document of financial control by not-for-profit organizations varies with the size of the organization and, to some extent, with the type of services that the organization provides. However, there are some basic principles that an organization might use concerning its budget and actual reported financial results that may be of interest to the analyst of the financial statements of a not-for-profit organization. Here are some of these basic principles:

- *The annual budget presents too long of a time span to provide effective control.* The annual budget should be broken down into at least quarterly periods and, if not overly administratively burdensome, monthly periods. Dividing the annual budget by four quarters and twelve months is not always the best approach for all budgeted amounts. Any seasonality of the business of the not-for-profit organization should be taken into consideration in allocating an annual budget into shorter time frames.

- *Both revenues and expenses should be budgeted.* Where revenues are directly linked to expenses, the budget should contain consistent assumptions about both the revenue and the related expenses. For example, assume that a not-for-profit organization provides home health-care services under a grant with a local government that pays the organization based on the number of clients served. The budget would anticipate expenses based upon an estimated number of clients that would be served. The revenue budget should assume revenues based on the same number of clients served as was used in the expense side of the budget.

- *Periodic comparisons of budget to actual results must be made promptly and differences must be acted on where warranted.* This principle is the primary reason why a budget discussion is included in a chapter on financial analysis. If the budgeted amounts are not compared to the actual results in time for action to be taken by the not-for-profit organization, the effectiveness of the budget as a financial control tool is seriously diminished. The idea is not to adopt an annual budget and hope for the best. The idea is to adopt an annual budget and take whatever actions are necessary to prevent deviations from the budget that would harm the not-for-profit organization. For example, if travel expenses are way over budget for the first six months of the year, travel for the balance of the year should be curtailed. If contribution revenue is falling behind the budgeted amounts, perhaps efforts can be increased to improve these revenues or perhaps some expenses need to be cut to maintain balance in the budget. Whatever the action needed, not acting on problems highlighted by a timely comparison of the budget to actual results is a terrible waste of an effective financial management tool.

- *Overly optimistic revenue and expense projections should be avoided.* To some extent, the budget to actual comparisons described in the previous bullet will discourage this practice, but it is sometimes hard for management of not-for-profit organizations to avoid being overly optimistic in their estimates of contributions and other revenues and how much expenses can be curtailed. Being too optimistic means that a not-for-profit organization will need to adjust during the year to make up for revenue shortfalls or expense overruns, and this is almost always not only disruptive but also counterproductive to the organization.

- *A reasonable process to allow the not-for-profit organization to modify its budget should be in place.* Small changes and shifting of small amounts between categories of revenues and expenses may be left to the discretion of management. Other more significant changes should not be done without the approval of the board of directors or its budget and finance committee. It is literally impossible for a not-for-profit organization to know what will happen during a new fiscal year as it prepares its budget for that year—new program initiatives may arise, an unexpectedly large contribution may be received, a grant from a private foundation may be won, and so on. How to handle significant increases or decreases in resources should be addressed in a budget modification process.

Many not-for-profit organizations will already incorporate some or all of these budget techniques and principles. The purpose of the above is not to present a checklist of practices for not-for-profit organizations to adopt. It is meant to propose a list of ideas that a non-accountant might use to understand and critique a not-for-profit organization's budget control process. Particularly when the non-accountant is a member of the not-for-profit organization's board of directors and has fiduciary responsibilities to the organization, being comfortable with the budget control process and knowing some best practices in this area can be very helpful.

SUMMARY

One important purpose of learning about GAAP for not-for-profit organizations is so that the financial statements of these organizations can be read with enough knowledge to allow the reader to ask some good questions and really understand the financial operations and financial position of the organization. Relating actual financial results with the annual budgets that are adopted by the vast majority of not-for-profit organizations is important in understanding how the budget is used as a means of financial management. It also helps the reader understand how budgeted financial amounts drive the financial results of not-for-profit organizations that are ultimately reported in their financial statements.

CHAPTER 12

Current Developments in Not-for-Profit GAAP

It is important for the non-accountant to understand that GAAP, including GAAP for not-for-profit organizations, is not static—it is constantly changing. Sometimes these changes are broad and have a significant impact on accounting and financial reporting. Other times these changes represent a tweaking of current requirements or are new rules that are the result of new types of transactions or economic events.

The purpose of this chapter is to highlight for the reader the more recent developments in accounting as they relate to not-for-profit organizations. Remember also that GAAP is based on various types of statements, standards, and pronouncements from more than one source. As the discussion of this GAAP hierarchy described in Chapter 1 points out, statements issued by the FASB are at the highest level in the GAAP hierarchy and, thus, will form the largest part of the coverage provided in this chapter. However, pronouncements and publications from other sources, particularly the American Institute of Certified Public Accountants, will also be included. Specifically, this chapter provides summarized information on:

- Recent FASB Statements
- AICPA Exposure Draft on Accounting for Certain Costs and Activities Related to Property, Plant, and Equipment

• FASB Project on Not-for-Profit Business Combinations

The reader interested in the status of these projects sequent to the publication of this book can look at the FASB's Web site (www.fasb.org).

RECENT FASB STATEMENTS

The following are summaries of the most recent FASB statements issued about the time of the publication of this book:

FASB Statement No. 141, "Business Combinations"

Summary: This statement specifies the accounting for business combinations. It eliminates the use of the pooling-of-interest method of accounting for these transactions, and requires the use of the purchase method of accounting for these transactions. Most importantly, it does not apply to combinations between not-for-profit organizations, nor does it apply to the acquisition of a for-profit business entity by a not-for-profit organization.

Effective Date: Not applicable to not-for-profit organizations.

FASB Statement No. 142, "Goodwill and Other Intangible Assets"

Summary: This statement significantly changes the way that not-for-profit organizations account for intangible assets. Intangible assets are those assets (other than financial assets) that lack physical substance. Examples would include copyrights, patents, trademarks, franchises, and service marks.

Intangible assets that are acquired or obtained are recorded on the statement of financial position as an asset. SFAS 142 specifies when costs related to intangible assets should be charged to expense rather than recorded as an asset. It specifies that costs of internally developing, maintaining, or restoring intangible assets that are not specifically identifiable, that have indeterminate lives, or that are inherent in a continuing business and related to an entity as a whole are recognized as an expense when incurred. For example, if a college buys a franchise from an international chain to operate a gourmet coffee shop on campus, it would record the franchise fee as an intangible asset. However, if it later incurs costs to maintain the value of its intangible asset (sponsors a campus 5K race and hands out T-shirts with the store's logo on it), this cost relates to maintaining the value of its intangible asset and would be expensed when incurred.

Under SFAS 142, intangible assets are classified as those that have finite useful lives and those that have indefinite lives. If the intangible asset has a finite life, it is amortized (that is, systematically charged to expense) over its useful life. The organization should consider whether the value of this asset has become impaired, as it would for other assets, as described in Chapter 1.

If the intangible asset has an infinite life, the organization would not amortize the asset. This is the major change from previous accounting since, prior to SFAS 142, all intangible assets had to be amortized, even if their life was indefinite. Intangible assets that are not subject to amortization are required to be tested for impairment at least annually and even more frequently if events or changes in circumstances indicate that the asset might be impaired.

The reader might ask why the change was made from always requiring amortization of intangible assets to only requiring amortization when their lives are finite. The reason relates back to SFAS 141's requirement to use the purchase method of accounting for business combinations. The purchase method of accounting often results in the recording of an intangible asset called goodwill. Goodwill did not arise from business combinations accounted for by the pooling-of-interests method. Businesses were furious that they would be required to use a method that resulted in the recording of goodwill, since the subsequent amortization of goodwill would hurt their reported earnings. Since goodwill has an indefinite life, amortization will not be required, which softens businesses' objections to SFAS 141. Although not-for-profit organizations are not directly impacted by SFAS 141, they are affected by its companion statement, SFAS 142.

Effective date: The basic effective date of SFAS 142 is for fiscal years beginning after December 15, 2001.

FASB Statement No. 143, "Accounting for Asset Retirement Obligations"

Summary: This statement started as a project requested of the FASB to issue accounting guidance for liabilities expected to be incurred for decommissioning nuclear power plants. The scope of the project was expanded to include all legal obligations associated with the retirement of any tangible long-lived asset that results from acquisition, construction, or development.

If an organization has a legal obligation that arises from the retirement of a long-lived asset, it should recognize a liability for this obligation in its statement of financial position in the year that the liability is incurred, provided that a reasonable estimate of the fair value of the liability can be made. When the liability is recorded, there is no corresponding expense immediately recorded. Rather, the same amount that is recorded as a liability is added to the recorded cost of the long-lived asset. This cost is then allocated to expense over the asset's useful live, which basically means that a higher depreciation expense is recorded in subsequent years to reflect the systematic expensing of the capitalized asset retirement obligation.

Effective date: SFAS 143 is effective for financial statements issued for fiscal years beginning after June 30, 2002.

FASB PROJECT ON NOT-FOR-PROFIT COMBINATIONS

One of the more important accounting statements that will affect not-for-profit organizations on the FASB horizon is a statement on the accounting for combinations of not-for-profit organizations.

Guidance is needed in this area because, until now, not-for-profit organizations generally accounted for the combination of two organizations using the pooling-of-interests method of accounting mentioned earlier. This method basically results in adding together the book values of the recorded assets and liabilities of the two organizations to arrive at the financial statements of the combined organization. Since SFAS 141 eliminated the pooling-of-interests method as an acceptable practice, there is a void in guidance for accounting for combinations of not-for-profit organizations. The purchase method of accounting does not seem to be a good fit for accounting for combinations of not-for-profit organizations, since these transactions usually do not involve the transfer of cash or securities that would provide a fair value to the "acquired" organizations. Not-for-profit organizations usually just combine their operations without an exchange of cash or other consideration.

At the time of this writing, the FASB is still drafting an Exposure Draft of a new statement that will provide accounting guidance in this area. However, the FASB has indicated that it has reached some preliminary conclusions about how it intends to specify the accounting for these transactions. These preliminary conclusions are, of course, subject to change as the FASB deliberates the contents of the Exposure Draft and then deliberates a final statement.

The FASB has indicated that it has made the following decisions regarding the accounting for a combination of two not-for-profit organizations in which the acquiring organization can be identified and when no cash or other assets are exchanged as consideration:

- The combination of two not-for-profit organizations as described above should be accounted for by the acquiring organization in a manner similar to a contribution under SFAS 116. The contribution should be measured in the financial statements as the total of the fair value of the identifiable assets acquired and the fair value of the liabilities assumed. The assets and liabilities acquired should be recorded in the financial statements at their fair values. The excess of assets acquired over the liabilities assumed would be recognized as a contribution received.

- If the total of the fair values of the liabilities assumed exceeds the fair values of the identifiable assets acquired (which is expected to be rare), the acquiring not-for-profit organization would recognize the difference as an unidentifiable intangible asset, which would be considered goodwill.

Guidance will be provided as to how to identify the acquiring organization in a combination of two not-for-profit organizations. The FASB has made these preliminary decisions:

- In determining the acquiring organization, all pertinent facts and circumstances are to be considered, in particular, whether one of the combining organizations has the ability to dominate the process of selecting a voting majority of the combined organization's initial governing board. In determining whether one of the combining organizations has the ability to dominate the selection process, consideration would be given to:
  - The existence of rights provided by the combined organiza-tion's articles of incorporation, its bylaws, or by provisions in the combination agreement to appoint members to the combined organization's governing body, and
  - The ability to dominate that process by other means.
- The anticipated Exposure Draft will provide implementation guidance, which will list a series of factors to consider in identifying the acquiring organization.

Certain combinations of two not-for-profit organizations include the exchange of cash or other assets as consideration. In addition, not-for-profit organizations sometimes acquire a business enterprise. The FASB has made the following preliminary decisions regarding these types of transactions:

- The combination should be accounted for by the acquiring enterprise similar to that required by SFAS 141. However, the facts and circumstances surrounding the combination should be reviewed to assess whether the combination is a transaction that is in part an exchange transaction and in part a contribution. If the facts and circumstances provide clear evidence that there is a contribution inherent in the transaction, that contribution received should be recognized by the acquiring organization in accordance with SFAS 116. The FASB has identified two examples of facts and circumstances that provide evidence that the combination is one that is in part an exchange transaction and in part a contribution:
    - The total of the fair values of the assets acquired and liabilities assumed exceeds the fair value of the consideration exchanged, particularly if the amount of this excess is substantial in relation to the fair value of the net assets acquired and no unstated rights or privileges are involved.
    - A review of the facts and circumstances surrounding the combination, including careful study of the negotiations, provides evidence that the participants were acting as a donor and a donee and as a buyer and a seller.

AICPA EXPOSURE DRAFT ON ACCOUNTING FOR CERTAIN COSTS AND ACTIVITIES RELATED TO PROPERTY, PLANT, AND EQUIPMENT

The AICPA has issued an Exposure Draft of a Proposed Statement of Position on Accounting for Certain Costs and Activities Related to Property, Plant, and Equipment (proposed SOP). When this Exposure Draft is finalized, the FASB is expected to issue a new statement, which will update several of its current statements to conform with the new SOP. The SOP provides guidance as to when to capitalize costs incurred relating to property, plant, and equipment.

The following are the definitions and accounting requirements as contained in the proposed SOP, which identifies four stages in which costs may be incurred relative to property, plant, and equipment:

Preliminary Stage

During the preliminary stage, an entity's activities include exploration of various opportunities for acquisition or construction of property, plant, and equipment. An entity may conduct feasibility studies and other activities related to asset selection. The entity may incur costs to obtain an option to acquire one or more items of property, plant, and equipment during this stage. Examples of other costs that may be incurred include surveying, zoning, engineering studies, design layouts, traffic studies, and costs associated with obtaining management's approval to move forward with particular property, plant, and equipment acquisition or construction.

Preacquisition Stage

During the preacquisition stage, certain of an entity's activities and kinds of costs incurred may be similar to those activities and costs incurred during the preliminary stage except that in the preacquisition stage they occur after it is probable that the entity will acquire specific property, plant, and equipment.

Acquisition-or-Construction Stage

The third stage, the acquisition-or-construction stage, begins at the time the entity obtains ownership of the property, plant, and equipment or obtains the right to use the property, plant, and equipment through an agreement (for example, a lease). During this stage, acquisition, construction, or installation activities related to the property, plant, and equipment occur. Examples of those activities include planning for construction or installation once ownership, or the right to use, has been acquired; constructing or installing property, plant, and equipment; and supervising the construction or acquisition of property, plant, and equipment.

In-Service Stage

The fourth and final stage, the in-service stage, commences when the property, plant, and equipment is substantially complete and ready for its intended use. Costs incurred during this stage relate principally to replacements, repairs, and maintenance, but may also include relocation costs.

The proposed SOP requirements include:

- Preliminary stage costs, except for payments to obtain an option to acquire property, plant, and equipment, should be charged to expense as incurred.
- Preacquisition and acquisition-or-construction stage costs should be charged to expense as incurred unless the costs are directly identifiable with the specific property, plant, and equipment. Directly identifiable costs include only:
  - Incremental direct costs of activities incurred in transactions with independent third parties for the specific property, plant, and equipment.
  - Certain costs directly related to specified activities performed by the entity for the specific property, plant, and equipment.
  - Payments to obtain an option to acquire property, plant, and equipment.
- Costs related to property, plant, and equipment that are incurred during the in-service stage, including costs of normal, recurring, or periodic repairs and maintenance activities, should be charged to expense as incurred unless the costs are incurred for (1) the acquisition of additional property, plant, and equipment or components of property, plant, and equipment or (2) the replacement of exist-

ing property, plant, and equipment or components of property, plant, and equipment.

- Removal costs incurred during replace of property, plant, and equipment, except for certain demolition costs, should be charged to expense as incurred.
- During all stages, general and administrative costs and overhead costs, including costs of support functions, should be charged to expense as incurred.
- Costs of planned major maintenance activities are not a separate property, plant, and equipment asset or component. Those costs should be charged to expense, except for acquisitions or replacements of components that are capitalizable under the in-service stage guidance of this SOP.

The requirements of the proposed SOP will likely result in a tightening of the requirements for when organizations, including not-for-profit organizations, will be able to capitalize costs relating to the acquisition or construction of property, plant, and equipment. In other words, it is likely that some of the costs described above that would be required to be charged to expense under the proposed SOP are probably currently being capitalized as part of the cost of the asset acquired or constructed under current accounting principles.

Effective Date: The proposed SOP indicates that the effective date of the final SOP will be for financial statements for fiscal years beginning after June 15, 2002.

SUMMARY

In understanding GAAP for not-for-profit organizations, it is important to keep one eye on the horizon for accounting requirements that are new or likely to be finalized in the near future. Not-for-profit organizations can use this information to plan for upcoming accounting rules and the impacts that they will have on their financial statements. These potential impacts should also be considered for how they affect (or should affect) a not-for-profit organization's budget.

Index